BLOODAXE POETRY INTRODUCTIONS

1

edited by
NEIL ASTLEY

BLOODAXE BOOKS

ISBN: 1 85224 731 2

First published 2006 by
Bloodaxe Books Ltd,
Highgreen,
Tarset,
Northumberland NE48 1RP.

www.bloodaxebooks.com
For further information about Bloodaxe titles
please visit our website or write to
the above address for a catalogue.

Bloodaxe Books Ltd acknowledges
the financial assistance of
Arts Council England, North East.

SPECIAL THANKS
To Alison Davis, especially, for thinking up this series,
and to Kennet Havgaard for his portraits used on the covers
(of people unconnected with the books or authors featured).

Cover printing by J. Thomson Colour Printers Ltd, Glasgow.

Printed in Great Britain by
Bell & Bain Limited, Glasgow, Scotland.

CONTENTS

ELIZABETH ALEXANDER

7 *Introduction*
9 Interview with Elizabeth Alexander *by* NATASHA TRETHEWEY
12 ELIZABETH ALEXANDER: *The Responsibilities of the Black Poet*
15 The Venus Hottentot
18 House Party Sonnet: '66
19 Boston Year
19 Affirmative Action Blues (1993)
21 After
22 Apollo
23 Race
23 1968
24 Gravitas
24 Crash
25 Peccant
26 Feminist Poem Number One
27 Little Slave Narrative #1: Master
27 Smile
28 Ars Poetic #92: Marcus Garvey on Elocution
29 Ars Poetic #100: I Believe
30 Translator

MONIZA ALVI

31 *Introduction*
32 MONIZA ALVI: *The Least International Shop in the World*
37 I Was Raised in a Glove Compartment
37 I Would Like to Be a Dot in a Painting by Miró
38 Throwing Out My Father's Dictionary
38 Indian Cooking
39 Presents from My Aunts in Pakistan
41 Arrival 1946
41 The Country at My Shoulder
42 The Sari
43 And If
44 The Wedding
45 Houdini
46 Carrying My Wife
47 Man Impregnated
47 The International Stores
48 The Other Family
49 Presents
50 The Other Room
50 How the World Split in Two

51 How a Long Way Off Rolled Itself Up
51 How the Children Were Born
52 Half-and-Half
52 Rural Scene

IMTIAZ DHARKER

53 *Introduction*
55 *from* Interview with Imtiaz Dharker *by* MENKA SHIVDASANI
58 Imtiaz Dharker's Art: Interview *by* ALEXANDRA HAMLYN
59 Blessing
59 Purdah I
60 Postcards from god I
61 Living Space
62 Minority
63 The Name of god
64 Honour killing
65 Front door
66 They'll say, 'She must be from another country'
68 This room
68 Platform
69 The terrorist at my table
70 Campsie Fells
72 Before I
72 These are the times we live in I
74 How to cut a pomegranate

JACKIE KAY

75 *Introduction*
77 Interview with Jackie Kay *by* LAURA SEVERIN
80 JACKIE KAY *writes*
81 *from* The Adoption Papers
83 Dance of the Cherry Blossom
85 Pounding Rain
86 The Red Graveyard
87 Blues
88 Twelve Bar Bessie
89 In my country
90 Hottentot Venus
91 Somebody Else
91 Pride
93 Things Fall Apart
94 Late Love
95 It's You and Me Baby All the Way to the End of the Line
95 Old Tongue
96 Life Mask

ELIZABETH ALEXANDER

FENAN SAMUEL

Elizabeth Alexander is a leading American poet whose work has been inspired by a wide range of influence, from history, literature, art and music, dreams and stories to the 'rich infinity' of the African American experience. Hers is a vital and vivid poetic voice on race, gender, politics and motherhood. Many of her poems bring history alive and singing into the present in highly musical, sharply contemporary narratives which use many different forms and voices to cover subjects ranging from slave rebellions, the Civil Rights movement, Muhammed Ali and Toni Morrison to the lives of jazz musicians and the 'Venus Hottentot', a 19th-century African woman exhibited at carnivals (Saartjie Bartmaan, also the subject of a poem by Jackie Kay, written around the same time: see page 89).

She has published four collections of poetry in the US, *Venus Hottentot* (1990), *Body of Life* (1996), *Antebellum Dream Book* (2001) and *American Sublime* (2005), as well as a book of essays on African American artistic life through literature, painting, film and popular media, *The Black Interior* (Graywolf Press, 2004). Her first British publication, *American Blue: Selected Poems* (Bloodaxe Books, 2006), draws on all these. Her verse play, *Diva Studies*, premièred at the

7

Yale School of Drama in 1996. The selection of her poems here includes work from all the collections covered by *American Blue*. The final poem, 'Translator', is from her long sequence *Amistad* (in *American Sublime*) about a rebellion in 1839 aboard a Spanish schooner taking slaves from Africa to Cuba; the ship was seized by the US Navy and taken to New Haven, Connecticut, but after a series of trials and appeals, the captives were eventually freed and returned to Sierra Leone.

Elizabeth Alexander was born in 1962 in Harlem, New York, grew up in Washington, DC, and studied at the universities of Yale, Boston and Pennsylvania. She lives in New Haven, Connecticut, and is Professor of African-American Studies at Yale University. She has received many awards, including, mostly recently, an inaugural Alphonse Fletcher, Sr Award for work 'that contributes to improving race relations in American society'.

SOME RESPONSES TO ELIZABETH ALEXANDER'S WORK:

'These poems of personal history are so particular in the rendering and so precisely made that they often transcend the poet's private domain and stand beautifully for the human condition in all its glory and tragedy. In other words, Alexander has an instinct for turning her profound cultural vision into one that illuminates universal experience' – CLARENCE MAJOR.

'In narratives sweetened by the lyric pulse and pierced through by felicitous turns of irony, Alexander chronicles the world of "black and tan". Her poems bristle with the irresistible quality of a world seen fresh. Race is present in her poems in the way that sex, class, age, even weather are present in all of our lives' – RITA DOVE, *Washington Post*.

'Alexander is an unusual thing, a sensualist of history, a romanticist of race. She weaves biography, history, experience, pop culture and dream. Her poems make the public and private dance together' – *Chicago Tribune*.

'*Antebellum Dream Book*...uses the structure of dreams to meditate about the strangeness of race, the mysteries of family, the centrality of African American precursors, and the excitements – and estrangements – of motherhood' – EDWARD HIRSCH.

'Alexander uses exquisite care and delicacy to explore turbulent times and feelings, Bravo!' – NTOZAKE SHANGE.

8

Interview with Elizabeth Alexander
by NATASHA TRETHEWEY

NT: What was growing up in Washington like? Did it have an effect on your work?

EA: Washington was a great place during the 60s and 70s. I grew up surrounded by electoral politics as well as the street politics and protests of the late 60s. The 1963 March on Washington was an often invoked benchmark of my family's move from New York to that city. Washington's disfranchisement was a vital issue throughout my childhood, and my father was a candidate in the city's first mayoral election in 1974. So a sense of national issues played out on a local stage, and vice versa, and of private lives made public was a part of my upbringing.

Washington is also an international city, and an internationally black city. My childhood awareness of the rest of the black world was sometimes imprecise, but omnipresent, and my much admired and adored late grandmother was proudly an "internationalist" who grew up in D.C. as well and roller-skated to the embassies 'to see that the rest of the world was there', as I write in 'Feminist Poem Number One'. I think that curiosity about the black world beyond my black city, and how I fit into it all, is important to my work, even when inexplicit.

My parents are New Yorkers – more specifically Harlemites, which is where I was born – and that is a fierce identity that never leaves you. I feel lucky not to have been too circumscribed by localness – any localness can have its limitations – to have something else to belong to and to fantasise about as well, which you see in many mentions of New York in my poems. I seem to be very interested in "real" or "natural" identities and their tug with constructed ones, and the romance of racial and geographic identification.

NT: You have a poem in your collection *Antebellum Dream Book* called 'Race'. Reading the poem, and particularly the last two lines – 'What a strange thing is race and family stranger still. / Here a poem tells a story, a story about race' – I get a glimpse of not only your thoughtfulness, but also your sense of humor. It's as if you said, 'Okay, I'm going to deal with it once and for all – here's the banner title.' Can you talk about the role race plays in your work?

EA: There are great storytellers in my family, as in so many of our families. But sometimes it's rare that those stories are transportable

9

or translatable intact into poem form; somebody talking to you is not the same as how you would tell a story or use narrative in a poem. These stories about color and about passing and even about siblings and their adult relationships and the readjustments of their adult relationships, as you have in that poem are the stones that so many of us have and do tell or don't tell.

As for the 'banner headline', 'Race', I always loved the way that my grandfather, and to a lesser extent my parents, used the word *race* to talk about 'the race' – meaning, of course, black people – as a thing that they could imagine, a body of people that we could imagine, that you could almost get your arms around, that the race was something tangible and palpable. I think it is in some very important ways generational. I also thought about the idea of what it meant to be a 'race man' or a 'race woman', what it meant to 'do something for the race', or what it meant to 'bring shame upon the race'.

NT: You've written some successful persona poems about historical personae. How do you go about making their voices real, as in 'The Venus Hottentot', which is about Saartjie Baartman?

EA: With invented voices, how do we really know if they are accurate or not? There's no way of knowing. Certainly in writing 'The Venus Hottentot', one of the big challenges was to hold on, especially when the Venus Hottentot herself speaks, because that's a longer part of the poem – to create a voice, and then to hold on to it and keep it consistent when it was not a voice that felt close to my own.

NT: You make it look effortless, though.

EA: Oh, I labored! [*Laughter*] To really, really be tight and to strike the proper historical note and tone, I did a lot of historical research, though there wasn't a lot to be found about Saartjie Bartmaan at the time. But I read about carnivals and circuses and London in the early 19th century, and all kinds of different things that would give me a sense of her world. I didn't want to be anachronistic, although at the same time there are very deliberately anachronistic moments – for example at the end, when she imagines her daughters in banana skirts and ostrich-feather fans, which is alluding to a Josephine Baker act, not something that she would have known. But that is where poetic license comes in handy.

I think in a poem like 'Race', in a way, I'm speaking in a voice that is more familiar. Certainly that, too, is a very formal poem in its way. It has a set of rules that it follows, but it's trying to be a little chattier, a little more contemporary. The speaker is a contemporary

10

person like myself telling a story, with the things that I know and my vocabulary to call upon. What I've always been interested in about 'The Venus Hottentot', and what I think is such a great teaching tool about persona poems, is that if you write about a character who obsesses you, you might not even know necessarily why that character is so compelling to you. Much later, after writing 'The Venus Hottentot', I thought, 'Well, of course I know about being a black woman who is the subject of objectification, who is in some people's eyes a spectacle simply for being a black woman, who is in some people's eyes sexualised simply for being a black woman.' That's something that we all know as black women in the world.

NT: In your third collection, *Antebellum Dream Book*, did you find yourself taking uncertain paths? And did much of the book's surreal imagery come from actual dreams you were having?

EA: Much of it did; some of it didn't. Obviously, much of it was made possible by first trusting the surreal images that came out of actual dreams. I've been lucky to always have been a really great dreamer. And I've always been fascinated by my own dreams and the dreams of others, what different cultures believe about dreams: how they guide you, how they tell you things that you should pay attention to, how they sometimes look ahead to the future, how they're a place where the ancestors can come and speak to you. So I've used dreams before in poems, but I just went further this time, really trusting that these strange juxtapositions could work as poetry.

NT: So you aren't afraid to trust that kind of surreal dream imagery to take you to new places?

EA: Well, I have a great fear of getting stuck in a rut. I think there are certain kinds of poems – such as poems in the 'Venus Hottentot' mode, poems that engage a black historical figure, an aspect of black history – that I sort of know how to do, and that I feel I can do well. I don't want to do that kind of poem to death, although certainly there's so much to write about in that whole area. That's just to say I wouldn't want to be someone who just writes the same version of a poem she wrote before over and over and over again. That would be the worst thing.

NT: Your first book begins with a poem that imagines the voice of a woman who has been objectified and thus rendered a mere body. Then you have a second collection entitled *The Body of Life*; and your next collection, *Antebellum Dream Book*, seemed to deal with the body in many more ways. In your work, what does it mean to 'write the body'?

11

EA: I think, certainly for women, that the stories of so many bodies are not the stories that we have heard. I remember once, teaching Descartes, one of my feminist colleagues saying that she asked the class, 'If Descartes were a woman who had given birth, would he have written "I think, therefore I am"?' In other words, what would a more embodied version of that statement look like? What that means to me is 'What would so many versions of our history look like if the body of the physically abused woman, the body of the sexually exulting woman, the body of the child-birthing woman, the body of the slave, the body of the domestic worker all spoke and told their stories and narrated their embodied experiences?' That's a huge, vast terrain. If you let a body speak, it gives you access to all sorts of concrete sensations that are vital, the stuff of poetry, the way a poem *convinces*. When my oldest child began to realise that he smelled things, he started telling me what everything smelled like: 'Oh, it smells like toast in here' or 'Oh, it smells like sickness in here'. He'd go through experiencing the world only through smell. What a gift to go through life being aware that we've been given these senses and that you should live in them: something to look at, something to smell, something to taste – all as a gift.

Extract from 'The Far, Deep Things of Dreamland: an interview with Elizabeth Alexander' by Natasha Trethewey, from *Poets & Writers* (Nov-Dec 2001).

ELIZABETH ALEXANDER

The Responsibilities of the Black Poet

At the first Fisk Black Writers' Conference in 1966, black writers defining the aims for a new black awareness clashed with the poet Robert Hayden. Responding to the country's ambient urgency, those writers wanted work that 'promote[d] an aesthetic that furthered the cause of black revolution'. But Hayden insisted that, when it came to his writing, he was a poet first and black, second. In 1978, he re-stated his view:

> To put it succinctly, I feel that Afro-American poets ought to be looked at as poets first, if that's what they truly are. And as one of them I dare to hope that if my work means anything, if it's any good at all, it's going to have a human impact, not a narrowly racial or ethnic or political and overspecialised impact.

The battle for the eloquent words of black writers to further the cause for black dignity and Civil Rights was on. [...]

Langston Hughes's 1926 essay 'The Negro Artist and the Racial Mountain' offers perennially resonant words that name necessary freedoms for black artists. This anthem bears quoting at length:

> We younger Negro artists who create now intend to express our individual dark-skinned selves without fear or shame. If white people are pleased we are glad. If they are not, it doesn't matter. We know we are beautiful. And ugly too. The tom-tom cries and the tom-tom laughs. If colored people are pleased we are glad. If they are not, their displeasure doesn't matter either. We build our temples for tomorrow, strong as we know how, and we stand on top of the mountain, free within ourselves.

Black writers know well the perils of white racism and racist judgements against us and our work. Racism is a straightforward, if unpleasant, navigation for any African American. But we are also, as ever, faced with judgements and injunctions from within our community that our work should perform a certain service as well as say and not say what is empowering or embarrassing to 'the race' at large. The pressure on creative work can be intense for artists who belong to groups still struggling for their fair shake in society. The challenges to be published and heard, let alone to write well, lead to the understandable conclusion that every word counts. Those who wish for justice for the race would also wish their words could further the cause, however controversially that cause might be defined. [...]

The expectations placed on black poets by a larger public are one thing. The demands of one's own people – however vexing it can be to draw perimeters around that populace – have always been another. What does the race want from its poets? Different and usually unpredictable things, in my experience, and often nothing but the particular vision a particular poet has to offer. Who is 'the race', anyway? Yes, there are literary schools and establishments, but certainly no central committee deciding who is "in" and who is "out". Calibrating these influences is close to impossible, inevitably imprecise, and drains good energy from the work of writing poetry.

But I am sure I am not alone in wanting my own work to be useful, to find a voice that speaks to people and communities beyond myself. I have seen my work overpraised by narrow-minded white critics who seem relieved that some of my references and formal choices are familiar to their own cultural milieu. I have seen my work criticised small-mindedly by more than one black woman elder poet – the same poets I imagined would be pleased by it. Many audiences I read to are mostly segregated; I've been greeted with silences both appalled and appreciative by white audiences, been met with suspicious stares and raucous love by black audiences. I've been left out of anthologies and gatherings where I felt I should have been included and included where I felt my work couldn't possibly belong. I am most often surprised by who finds and appreciates my work, and for what reasons. I believe that poetry readers are largely eclectic and single-minded.

But the love that has meant the most, I have to say, has come from the diverse black communities who I feel "get it" on myriad levels, who see what I am trying to do with words and with message. I do not seek their approval when I write, but it pleases me when it comes, to echo and revise Hughes. I do not consider it a betrayal of my muse to say there are a few poems that I might write but not read or publish in certain forums because I felt – imagined? – they would cause harm to that amorphous group called black people, poems that might perpetuate dangerous stereotypes if taken drastically out of context. How many African Americans have modified what and where we say or do because we think it would reflect badly on 'the race'? What if these considerations do not make us prudish but rather indicate that there are familiar issues and degrees of self-censorship that we are faced with because of our history, and that our public acts are sometimes appropriately strategic? Such awareness can be separated from the fundamental work of internal liberation that is central to the poetic process.

Gwendolyn Brooks' *In the Mecca* (1968) taught me that none of us lives outside of historical moments or quotidian pressures and concerns. The historical challenge to understand context in which the elders of our tradition had to labor to make their voices heard is unusually pointed for black writers. Before the famous paragraph from 'The Negro Artist and the Racial Mountain', Hughes wrote something else that bears consideration. 'An artist must be free to choose what he does, certainly,' he wrote, 'but he must also never be afraid to do what he might choose.' Brooks never feared or shirked what she fervently believed was her responsibility; that sense of responsibility shaped her very aesthetic. Few poets walk with such integrity. Brooks's career in 1967 reminds us that the matter of listening to the muse, of being utterly 'free to choose', is always interrupted by larger concerns that can at times come to constitute the muse's voice. Whether those concerns are catalysts, straightjackets, or something in between is open to debate.

Extract from 'Meditations on "Mecca": Gwendolyn Brooks and the Responsibilities of the Black Poet', from *The Black Interior*.

The Venus Hottentot

(1825)

1 *Cuvier*

Science, science, science!
Everything is beautiful

blown up beneath my glass.
Colors dazzle insect wings.

A drop of water swirls
like marble. Ordinary

crumbs become stalactites
set in perfect angles

of geometry I'd thought
impossible. Few will

ever see what I see
through this microscope.

Cranial measurements
crowd my notebook pages,

and I am moving closer,
close to how these numbers

signify aspects of
national character.

Her genitalia
will float inside a labeled

pickling jar in the Musée
de l'Homme on a shelf

above Broca's brain:
'the Venus Hottentot'.

Elegant facts await me.
Small things in this world are mine.

15

2

There is unexpected sun today
in London, and the clouds that
most days sift into this cage
where I am working have dispersed.
I am a black cutout against
a captive blue sky, pivoting
nude so the paying audience
can view my naked buttocks.

I am called 'Venus Hottentot'.
I left Capetown with a promise
of revenue: half the profits
and my passage home: A boon!
Master's brother proposed the trip;
the magistrate granted me leave.
I would return to my family
a duchess, with watered-silk

dresses and money to grow food,
rouge and powders in glass pots,
silver scissors, a lorgnette,
voile and tulle instead of flax,
cerulean blue instead
of indigo. My brother would
devour sugar-studded non-
pareils, pale taffy, damask plums.

That was years ago. London's
circuses are florid and filthy,
swarming with cabbage-smelling
citizens who stare and query,
'Is it muscle? Bone? Or fat?'
My neighbor to the left is
The Sapient Pig, 'The Only
Scholar of His Race'. He plays

at cards, tells time and fortunes
by scraping his hooves. Behind
me is Prince Kar-mi, who arches
like a rubber tree and stares back
at the crowd from under the crook

of his knee. A professional
animal trainer shouts my cues.
There are singing mice here.

'The Ball of Duchess DuBarry':
In the engraving I lurch
toward the *belles dames*, mad-eyed, and
they swoon. Men in capes and pince-nez
shield them. Tassels dance at my hips.
In this newspaper lithograph
my buttocks are shown swollen
and luminous as a planet.

Monsieur Cuvier investigates
between my legs, poking, prodding,
sure of his hypothesis.
I half expect him to pull silk
scarves from inside me, paper poppies,
then a rabbit! He complains
at my scent and does not think
I comprehend, but I speak

English. I speak Dutch. I speak
a little French as well, and
languages Monsieur Cuvier
will never know have names.
Now I am bitter and now
I am sick. I eat brown bread,
drink rancid broth. I miss good sun,
miss Mother's *sadza*. My stomach

is frequently queasy from mutton
chops, pale potatoes, blood sausage.
I was certain that this would be
better than farm life. I am
the family entrepreneur!
But there are hours in every day
to conjure my imaginary
daughters, in banana skirts

and ostrich-feather fans.
Since my own genitals are public
I have made other parts private.

In my silence I possess
mouth, larynx, brain, in a single
gesture. I rub my hair
with lanolin, and pose in profile
like a painted Nubian

archer, imagining gold leaf
woven through my hair, and diamonds.
Observe the wordless Odalisque.
I have not forgotten my Khoisan
clicks. My flexible tongue
and healthy mouth bewilder
this man with his rotting teeth.
If he were to let me rise up

from this table, I'd spirit
his knives and cut out his black heart,
seal it with science fluid inside
a bell jar, place it on a low
shelf in a white man's museum
so the whole world could see
it was shriveled and hard,
geometric, deformed, unnatural.

House Party Sonnet: '66

Small, still. Fit through the banister slit.
Where did our love go? Where did our love go?
Scattered high heels and the carpet rolled back.
Where did our love go? Where did our love go?
My brother and I, tipping down from upstairs
Under the cover of 'Where Did Our Love Go?'
Cat-eyed Supremes wearing siren-green gowns.
Pink curls of laughter and hips when they shake
Shake a tambourine *where did our love go?*
Where did our love go? Where did our love go?
Stale chips next morning, shoes under the couch,
Smoke-smelling draperies, water-paled Scotch.
Matches, stray earrings to find and to keep –
Hum of invisible dancers asleep.

18

Boston Year

My first week in Cambridge a car full of white boys
tried to run me off the road, and spit through the window,
open to ask directions. I was always asking directions
and always driving: to an Armenian market
in Watertown to buy figs and string cheese, apricots,
dark spices and olives from barrels, tubes of paste
with unreadable Arabic labels. I ate
stuffed grape leaves and watched my lips swell in the mirror.
The floors of my apartment would never come clean.
Whenever I saw other colored people
in bookshops, or museums, or cafeterias, I'd gasp,
smile shyly, but they'd disappear before I spoke.
What would I have said to them? Come with me? Take
me home? Are you my mother? No. I sat alone
in countless Chinese restaurants eating almond
cookies, sipping tea with spoons and spoons of sugar.
Popcorn and coffee was dinner. When I fainted
from migraine in the grocery store, a Portuguese
man above me mouthed: 'No breakfast.' He gave me
orange juice and chocolate bars. The color red
sprang into relief singing Wagner's *Walküre*.
Entire tribes gyrated and drummed in my head.
I learned the samba from a Brazilian man
so tiny, so festooned with glitter I was certain
that he slept inside a filigreed, Fabergé egg.
No one at the door: no salesmen, Mormons, meter
readers, exterminators, no Harriet Tubman,
no one. Red notes sounding in a grey trolley town.

Affirmative Action Blues (1993)

Right now two black people sit in a jury room
in Southern California trying to persuade
nine white people that what they saw when four white
police officers brought batons back like
they were smashing a beautiful piñata was
'a violation of Rodney King's civil rights',

19

just as I am trying to convince my boss not ever
to use the word 'niggardly' in my presence again.
He's a bit embarrassed, then asks, but don't you know
the word's etymology? as if that makes it
somehow not the word, as if a word can't batter.
Never again for as long as you live, I tell him,
and righteously. Then I dream of a meeting
with my colleagues where I scream so loud the inside
of my skull bleeds, and my face erupts in scabs.
In the dream I use an office which is overrun
with mice, rats, and round-headed baby otters
who peer at me from exposed water pipes (and somehow
I know these otters are Negroes), and my boss says,
Be grateful, your office is bigger than anyone
else's, and maybe if you kept it clean you wouldn't
have those rats. And meanwhile, black people are dying,
beautiful black men my age, from AIDS. It was amazing
when I learned the root of 'venereal disease'
was 'Venus', that there was such a thing as a disease
of love. And meanwhile, poor Rodney King can't think straight;
what was knocked into his head was some addled notion
of love his own people make fun of, 'Can we all
get along? Please?' You can't hit a lick with a crooked
stick; a straight stick made Rodney King believe he was
not a piñata, that amor vincit omnia.
I know I have been changed by love.
I know that love is not a political agenda, it lacks sustained
analysis, and we can't dance our way out of our constrictions.
I know that the word 'niggardly' is 'of obscure etymology' but
        probably derived from the French Norman, and that
        Chaucer and Milton and Shakespeare used it. It means
        'stingy', and the root is not the same as 'nigger', which
        derives from 'negar', meaning black, but they are perhaps,
        perhaps, etymologically related. The two 'g's are two
        teeth gnawing; rodent is from the Latin 'rodere' which
        means 'to gnaw', as I have said elsewhere.
I know so many things, including the people who love me and the
        people who do not.
In Tourette's syndrome you say the very thing that you are thinking,
        and then a word is real.
These are words I have heard in the last 24 hours which fascinate
        me: 'vermin', 'screed', 'carmine', and 'niggardly'.
I am not a piñata, Rodney King insists. Now can't we all get along?

20

After

It wasn't as deep as I expected,
your grave, next to the grandmother who died
when I was three. I threw a flower in
and fizzled off the scene like carbonation.
My body of course remained but all else
was a cluster of tiny white bubbles
floating up, up, up, to an unseen top.

I wore your vicuna coat and an ill-
fitting cloche from Alexanders. I walked
among the rows, away from the men
covering the coffin, which was when I saw
'X', Malcolm, a few yards down, 'Paul Robeson',
then 'Judy Garland' then – the car was waiting
and we had to go.

The cocktail parties
must be something there! You'd discuss self-help
and the relative merits of Garvey-
ism with Malcolm. Robeson would read
in a corner. Judy, divine in black
clam-diggers, would throw back her head
and guffaw, smoke as many cigarettes
as she wanted.

Before you died I dreamed
of cocktail parties in your Harlem
apartment where you'd bring all our dead kin
back to life, for me! I was old enough
to drink with you, to wear a cocktail dress.
Like the best movies, the dream was black
and white, except for my grandmother's
lipstick, which was red.

Apollo

We pull off
to a road shack
in Massachusetts
to watch men walk

on the moon. We did
the same thing
for three two one
blast off, and now

we watch the same men
bounce in and out
of craters. I want
a Coke and a hamburger.

Because the men
are walking on the moon
which is now irrefutably
not green, not cheese,

not a shiny dime floating
in a cold blue,
the way I'd thought,
the road shack people don't

notice we are a black
family not from there,
the way it mostly goes.
This talking through

static, bouncing in space-
boots, tethered
to cords is much
stranger, stranger

even than we are.

Race

Sometimes I think about Great-Uncle Paul who left Tuskegee,
Alabama to become a forester in Oregon and in so doing
became fundamentally white for the rest of his life, except
when he traveled without his white wife to visit his siblings –
now in New York, now in Harlem, USA – just as pale-skinned,
as straight-haired, as blue-eyed as Paul, and black. Paul never told anyone
he was white, he just didn't say that he was black, and who could imagine,
an Oregon forester in 1930 as anything other than white?
The siblings in Harlem each morning ensured
no one confused them for anything other than what they were, black.
They were black! Brown-skinned spouses reduced confusion.
Many others have told, and not told, this tale.
When Paul came East alone he was as they were, their brother.

The poet invents heroic moments where the pale black ancestor stands up
on behalf of the race. The poet imagines Great-Uncle Paul
in cool, sagey groves counting rings in redwood trunks,
imagines pencil markings in a ledger book, classifications,
imagines a sidelong look from an ivory spouse who is learning
her husband's caesuras. She can see silent spaces
but not what they signify, graphite markings in a forester's code.

Many others have told, and not told, this tale.
The one time Great-Uncle Paul brought his wife to New York
he asked his siblings not to bring their spouses,
and that is where the story ends: ivory siblings who would not
see their brother without their telltale spouses.
What a strange thing is "race", and family, stranger still.
Here a poem tells a story, a story about race.

1968
(from 'Fugue')

The city burns. We have to stay at home,
TV always interrupted with fire or helicopters.
Men who have tweedled my cheeks once or twice
join the serial dead.

Yesterday I went downtown with Mom.
What a pretty little girl, said the tourists, who were white.
My shoes were patent leather, all shiny, and black.
My father is away saving the world for Negroes,
I wanted to say.

Mostly I go to school or watch television
with my mother and brother, my father often gone.
He makes the world a better place for Negroes.
The year is nineteen-sixty-eight.

Gravitas

Emergency! A bright yellow school bus
is speeding me to hospital. My pregnant belly bulges
beneath my pleated skirt, the face
of my dear niece Amal a locket inside my stomach.

Soon she will be born healthy,
and after, her sister, Bana.
Labor will be tidy and effortless.
In fact, I will hardly remember it!

All of this is taking place in Kenya, where they live.
This is my first dream of pregnancy
since I have been actually pregnant,
therefore I dream in reality rather than metaphor.

I am gravid, eight weeks along.
My baby, I have read, has a tail
and a spine made of pearls,
and every day I speak to her in tongues.

Crash

I am the last woman off of the plane
that has crashed in a cornfield near Philly,

picking through hot metal
for my rucksack and diaper bag.

No black box, no fuselage,
just sistergirl pilot wiping soot from her eyes,

happy to be alive. Her dreadlocks
will hold the smoke for weeks.

All the white passengers bailed out
before impact, so certain a sister

couldn't navigate the crash. O gender.
O race. O ye of little faith.

Here we are in the cornfield, bruised and dirty but alive.
I invite sistergirl pilot home for dinner

at my parents', for my mother's roast chicken
with gravy and rice, to celebrate.

Peccant

Maryland State Correctional Facility for Women,
Baltimore County Branch, has undergone a face-lift.
Cells are white and ungraffitied, roomlike, surprisingly airy.
This is where I must spend the next year, eating slop from tin trays,
facing women much tougher than I am, finding out if I am brave.
Though I do not know what I took, I know I took something.

On Exercise Day, walk the streets of the city you grew up in,
in my case, DC, from pillar to post, Adams-Morgan to Anacostia,
Shaw to Southwest, Logan to Chevy Chase Circles,
recalling every misbegotten everything, lamenting, repenting.

How my parents keen and weep, scheme to spring me,
intercept me at corners with bus tokens, pass keys, files baked in cakes.
Komunyakaa the poet says, don't write what you know,
write what you are willing to discover, so I will
spend this year, these long days, meditating on what I am accused of
in the white rooms, city streets, communal showers, mess hall,
where all around me sin and not sin is scraped off tin trays
into oversized sinks, all that excess, scraped off and rinsed away.

Feminist Poem Number One

Yes I have dreams where I am rescued by men:
my father, brother, husband, no one else.
Last night I dreamed my brother and husband
morphed into each other and rescued me
from a rat-infested apartment. 'Run!'
he said, feral scampering at our heels.
And then we went to lunch at the Four Seasons.

What does it mean to be a princess?
'I am what is known as an American Negro,'
my grandmother would say, when 'international friends'
would ask her what she was. She'd roller-skate
to Embassy Row and sit on the steps of the embassies
to be certain the rest of the world was there.

What does it mean to be a princess?
My husband drives me at 6 A.M.
to the airport an hour away, drives home,
drives back when I have forgotten my passport.
What does it mean to be a prince? I cook
savory, fragrant meals for my husband
and serve him, if he likes, in front of the TV.
He cooks for me, too. I have a husband.

In the dream we run into Aunt Lucy,
who is waiting for a plane from 'Abyssinia'
to bring her lover home. I am the one
married to an Abyssinian, who is already here. I am the one
with the grandmother who wanted to know the world.
I am what is known as an American Negro princess,
married to an African prince,
living in a rat-free apartment in New Haven,
all of it, all of it, under one roof.

Little Slave Narrative #1: Master

He would order the women to pull up their clothes
'in Alabama style', as he called it. He would whip them

for not complying. He taught bloodhounds
to chase down negro boys, hence the expression

'hell-hounds on my trail'. He was fond of peach brandy,
put ads in the paper: *Search high, search low*

for my runaway Isaac, my runaway Joe,
his right cheek scarred, occasioned by buckshot,

runaway Ben Fox, very black, chunky made,
two hundred dollars live, and if dead,

bring his dead body, so I may look at it.

Smile

When I see a black man smiling
like that, nodding and smiling
with both hands visible, mouthing

'Yes, Officer', across the street,
I think of my father, who taught us
the words 'cooperate', 'officer',

to memorise badge numbers,
who has seen black men shot at
from behind in the warm months north.

And I think of the fine line —
hairline, eyelash, fingernail paring —
the whisper that separates

obsequious from *safe*. Armstrong,
Johnson, Robinson, Mays.
A woman with a yellow head

of cotton candy hair stumbles out
of a bar at after-lunchtime
clutching a black man's arm as if

for her life. And the brother
smiles, and his eyes are flint
as he watches all sides of the street.

Ars Poetica #92: Marcus Garvey on Elocution

Elocution means to speak out.
That is to say, if you have a tale to tell,
tell it and tell it well.

This I was taught.

To speak properly you must have sound and good teeth.
You must have clear nostrils.
Your lungs must be sound.
Never try to make a speech on a hungry stomach.

Don't chew your words but talk them out plainly.
Always see that your clothing is properly arranged before you get on
*   a platform.*
You should not make any mistake in pronouncing your words
because that invites amusement for certain people.

To realise I was trained for this,
expected to speak out, to speak well.
To realise, my family believed
I would have words for others.

An untidy leader is always a failure.
A leader's hair should always be well kept.
His teeth must also be in perfect order.
Your shoes and other garments must also be clean.
If you look ragged, people will not trust you.

My father's shoe-shine box:
black Kiwi, cordovan Kiwi,
the cloths, the lambswool brush.

My grandmother's dressing table:
potions for disciplining
anything scraggle or stray.

For goodness sake, always speak out,
said Marcus Garvey,
said my parents,
said my grandparents,
and meant it.

Ars Poetica #100: I Believe

Poetry, I tell my students,
is idiosyncratic. Poetry

is where we are ourselves
(though Sterling Brown said

'Every "I" is a dramatic "I"'),
digging in the clam flats

for the shell that snaps,
emptying the proverbial pocketbook.

Poetry is what you find
in the dirt in the corner,

overhear on the bus, God
in the details, the only way

to get from here to there.
Poetry (and now my voice is rising)

is not all love, love, love,
and I'm sorry the dog died.

Poetry (here I hear myself loudest)
is the human voice,

and are we not of interest to each other?

Translator

(JAMES COVEY: *from 'Amistad'*)

I was stolen from Mendeland as a child
then rescued by the British ship *Buzzard*
and brought to Freetown, Sierra Leone.

I love ships and the sea, joined this crew
of my own accord, set sail as a teen,
now re-supplying in New York Harbor.

When the white professor first came to me
babbling sounds, I thought he needed help
until *weta*, my mother's six, hooked my ear

and I knew what he was saying, and I knew
what he wanted in an instant, for we had heard
wild tales of black pirates off New London,

the captives, the low black schooner like
so many ships, an infinity of ships fatted
with Africans, men, women, children

as I was. Now it is my turn to rescue.
I have not spoken Mende in some years,
yet every night I dream it, or silence.

To New Haven, to the jail. To my people.
Who am I now? This them, not them. We burst
with joy to speak and settle to the tale:

We killed the cook, who said he would cook us.
They rubbed gunpowder and vinegar in our wounds.
We were taken away in broad daylight.

And in a loud voice loud as a thousand waves
I sing my father's song. It shakes the jail.
I sing from my entire black body.

MONIZA ALVI

BOB COE

Moniza Alvi was born in Lahore, Pakistan, in 1954, the daughter of an English mother and a Pakistani father. Her family left for Britain when she was just a few months old, and she grew up in Hertfordshire, only returning to Pakistan in the mid-90s, after publishing her first book of poems, *The Country at My Shoulder* (1993). In this book and in her second collection, *A Bowl of Warm Air* (1996), she drew on real and imagined homelands in poems which are 'vivid, witty and imbued with unexpected and delicious glimpses of the surreal – this poet's third country' (Maura Dooley).

Ruth Padel has called her 'a bold surrealist, whose poems open the world up in new, imaginatively absurd ways', and Moniza Alvi has commented that her imagination has always been fed as much by 'fantasy and the strange-seeming' as by the strangeness of her background (see her essay 'The Least International Shop in the World').

Originally published by Oxford University Press, her first two collections were reprinted in her first Bloodaxe title, *Carrying My Wife* (2000), together with a third collection of new work. In her later poems, her delicately drawn fantasies transform the familiar into strange evocations of the joys and tensions of relationships, of

31

love, intimacy, frustration, jealousy and paranoia, exploring birth, death and parenthood as well as the fragility of life with a sure wit and lightness of touch.

In the title-sequence of *Carrying My Wife* (its title-poem and 'Man Impregnated' are included here), she plays the role of husband to an imaginary wife. In her essay she tells how, writing from a male or "husband" viewpoint, she was able both to distance herself and to zoom into sensations and difficulties, so that surreal aspects of relationships emerged as well as 'the humour which might have been blurred in a head-on approach'. These poems 'do not show a male stance, but another way of looking at oneself'.

Her delightfully paradoxical fourth collection, *Souls* (2002), is populated by troubled and troublesome souls who 'inhabit us as if our faces / were portraits in galleries – // and stare out of us / until they are tired of looking'...'We only know about life. / To the souls, / we're the real immortals.' Their escapades touch different facets of life and death, exploring tantalising dualities through delicious transformations; their moods and desires dart about on the edge of daily reality, revealing as much about ourselves as our own fantasies.

The title-sequence of *How the Stone Found Its Voice* (2005) is a series of poems inspired by creation myths. Begun in the wake of the tragedy of 9/11, they are imbued with the dark spirit of that time, with titles including 'How the World Split in Two' and 'How a Long Way Off Rolled Itself Up'.

A half-hour reading by Moniza Alvi is included on *The Poetry Quartets: 6* (The British Council/Bloodaxe Books, 2000).

After a long career as a secondary school teacher, Moniza Alvi now lives in south-west London with her husband and young daughter. She is a freelance writer, and a tutor for the the Poetry School. In 2002-04 she was a trainee at the Westminster Pastoral Foundation studying counselling and group analysis.

SOME RESPONSES TO MONIZA ALVI'S WORK:

'Much of Alvi's work engages with a surreal or fantastical world of fractured and partially recovered identity, working through sequences in her most recent poetry' – DERYN REES-JONES, *Modern Women Poets*.

'She is a skilled storyteller, recounting the extraordinary in the voice of the everyday, so that we accept the miraculous as something we need...the overriding impression is of a deft, restrained language carrying ideas with metaphysical wit and seriousness' – LEONIE RUSHFORTH, *London Magazine*.

MONIZA ALVI

The Least International Shop in the World

There used to be a shop in Hatfield, where I grew up, called The International Stores. My poem about it was inspired by something my mother said – that there didn't seem to be anything international about it at all. I remember that it was rather a posh shop for Hatfield, with a dignified atmosphere. There were impressive pyramids of tins, well-swept floors, and the cheddar and ham loomed large, presided over by the solemn shopkeeper. As words have connotations for us before we really think about their meanings, I probably gained the impression that 'international' was something to do with being more English than the English.

As I grew up in this Hertfordshire town in the 50s and 60s as a child with a mixed race background, there were few children in my situation. I was aware of one family of our acquaintance who seemed rather like us. They became the subject of another poem, 'The Other Family'. I marvelled at how dark the Ceylonese father was and how extremely pale his English wife seemed in comparison. I didn't consciously think that my parents might appear like this to observers. I envied the children because they had English names. It was startling to me, and in my poem the children carried 'their English names like snowballs'. I imagined my life would have been more straightforward if I'd been called Mandy, for example.

There was a great deal of racial invisibility at that time. The term "multicultural" was unknown to me and different backgrounds were not given focus at school or celebrated as they may well be now. I felt roughly the same as my classmates, but different – it was all very vague, and all the more so because I had an English mother and in many ways my family was very anglicised. Children do not like to be considered different and do their best to fit in, so on one level I was quite happy to consider myself *just the same as everybody else*. I would have half-accepted what some well-meaning teachers still say nowadays – 'I just teach children.' That is, *their origins are not important to me.*

I didn't begin writing poetry to explore my background. I had been writing seriously for several years before I started writing anything of my fantasies of Pakistan, and how the country made its impact on my early life. I read the poem 'The Bowl' by Mimi Khalvati and delighted in the richness of its imagery. It was soon after this that it occurred to me that I too had something to say about another culture. I didn't envisage a group of poems at first.

I wrote 'Indian Cooking' and, shortly afterwards, 'Presents from My Aunts in Pakistan', thinking that was all, but very soon further poems were pressing to be written, even when I'd decided that I really wanted to write about something else. But I was very excited because I'd chanced upon an area of writing that was my own unexplored territory. There was relief in at last making the invisible visible, and in creating something positive about what was, in childhood and adolescence, rather unsettling and difficult to think about.

This writing gave me the confidence to make my first return visit to Pakistan, which features in *A Bowl of Warm Air*: I felt that the opportunity to write would give me a way absorbing the experience – the extremity of the culture, and the alienation of meeting relatives who didn't speak English while I was unable to speak Urdu. Unsurprisingly, though disconcertingly, I have never felt so English as on that return trip to Pakistan. An overwhelming experience in many ways, the visit helped me to understand many aspects of my growing up, for instance, the family stress on education; a British education was still regarded as supreme.

When I entitled my first collection *The Country at My Shoulder* I thought of this country as not necessarily a geographic location, but as a reference to hidden worlds that can be entered through poetry. There's a danger in my being pigeonholed as a writer whose main concern is "Asian themes", though I do want that major aspect of my work to be valued. What concerns me is what is at the edge of the mind and can be brought to light and viewed from unusual angles. When I first started writing seriously I was reading Angela Carter, Italo Calvino, and J.G. Ballard's science fiction. I'm attracted by fantasy and the strange-seeming and find there some essence of experience. With its obliquely subversive power, fantasy links with the dream world and the unconscious. What was compelling about Pakistan was partly that I had no actual memories of it. Pakistan was a fantasy, nourished by vivid family stories, extraordinary gifts, letters, news items and anecdotes. In the poem 'The Sari', I imagine my mother in Lahore with a glass stomach, so that before I'm born I can look out and see what's going on around me. In her introduction to *Modern Women Poets* (2005), Deryn Rees-Jones draws attention to how various women writers use the surreal as 'a hinge between self and otherness', as with dreams, a way of saying the unsayable. I think this is now it functions for me.

Thus I wouldn't describe myself as a poet of place. I write about my experiences as broadly as I can, and my birthplace has been significant. I am aware that poetry I've written about my background has sometimes been rather different in style, even in mood from my other poems. Perhaps it's because Pakistan and my connection with the country strikes me as so surreal and fantastical in itself that I haven't quite got over it. Perhaps the country of my birth has become a symbol for other losses.

I was alarmed and disorientated, at first, to find myself almost metamorphosed overnight into a Black writer. I felt like an impostor, and as if other parts of me were being eclipsed. At a conference on Black writing, however, where I thought I would be very out of place, I was relieved to find other writers of mixed race present, such as Bernardine Evaristo, and to discover that the Black writer category was a broad one even if it could be somewhat misleading. Writers of novels and verse novels had comparable concerns to my own, although their voices were very different. Writing which portrayed growing up in London, and explored issues of race, was vibrant and very contemporary – essential reading, I hoped, for future readers in schools and colleges.

Poetry that reflects multicultural Britain is badly represented in the mainstream, particularly aspects of the Asian culture. I was delighted to read Meera Syal's novel *Anita and Me* about a girl growing up as the daughter of the only Punjabi family in a mining village near Wolverhampton in the 60s. Here was much with which I could identify, but I also find it inspiring to read poetry by writers from such backgrounds not necessarily specifically on "Asian themes". Recently I heard that one of my poems was included in a GCSE examination anthology under the section 'Poems from Other Cultures and Traditions'. This at once made me feel like an inhabitant of a distant corner of an empire. Surely the heading should be an inclusive 'Literature from Our Cultures'. It is good that school students are now studying a wider range of poetry than I was offered at school in the 60s, but it's important they don't receive messages that could reinforce a sense of their own lives as being "other", and marginalised.

The idea that my own life could be material for poetry didn't strike me at first. That is partly why I didn't start writing seriously until I was about 30 and was made aware of the unconscious and the symbolic richness of a dreamlife. Writing became an act of discovery on the border where inner and outer worlds meet, an attempt to extend myself and transform that which was constantly being taken in.

I'm often inspired to write by reading other poets' work, by their energy, freshness and inventiveness. Contemporary poets who've fired me include Vicki Feaver, Susan Wicks and Selima Hill. I feel an affinity with poets from a multicultural background, or those with a multiracial identity such as Mimi Khalvati, Sujata Bhatt and Imtiaz Dharker. I've been drawn to the work of Mark Strand and James Tate, and greatly admire poems by Louise Glück and Raymond Carver. The list is thankfully endless. If I couldn't read other poets' work, I wonder, would I continue?

When writing from personal experience I try to avoid heaviness and instead indulge in my own form of serious play. In the series *Carrying My Wife* I play the role of husband to an imaginary wife. In a sense the poems are autobiographical, and writing from a male or "husband" viewpoint has been a way of distancing myself from the sensations and difficulties portrayed, and then zooming in closely. I found surreal aspects of relationships emerged, and also the humour which might have been blurred in a head-on approach. In the end, I suppose, the poems do not show a male stance, but another way of looking at oneself. Poets may crave different voices. Shakespeare had men playing women playing men, as well as men playing lions. I've found it very satisfying and playful being a woman depicting a man, depicting a woman. This "bisexual" activity didn't feel at all artificial.

Some of my recent poems focus on the strange state of pregnancy and the responsibility of parenthood. I have also continued the investigations into my Pakistani background begun in my previous collections, this time touching on a kind of racial invisibility in the town where I grew up, and the "otherness" of growing up as a child of mixed origins. When we had elevenses in a department store, the waitress would ask 'How would you like your coffee?' and my mother would always say 'Half-and-half'. I was struck by this because I felt 'half-and-half' myself, and this memory prompted the poem 'Half-and-Half' where I explore my mixed identity. Pakistan was my father's country and the place where I was born and England my mother's country and where we lived; and Pakistan itself was a divided country then. More recently, after the tragedy for mankind of 9/11 in New York, it did seem as if the world itself was in danger of splitting in two, the Moslem world and the rest of the world. With my father's family in Pakistan, I found this very sad and confusing, and was prompted to write the series of short myth poems in my latest collection *How the Stone Found Its Voice* which include 'How the World Split in Two'.

Edited version of essay first published in *Contemporary Women's Poetry: Reading/Writing/Practice*, ed. Alison Mark & Deryn Rees-Jones (Macmillan, 2000).

I Was Raised in a Glove Compartment

I was raised in a glove compartment.
The gloves held out limp fingers –

in the dark I touched them.
I bumped against the First Aid tin,

and rolled on notepads and maps.
I never saw my mother's face –

sometimes
her gloved hand would reach for me.

I existed in the quiet – I listened
for the sound of the engine.

I Would Like to Be a Dot in a Painting by Miró

I would like to be a dot in a painting by Miró.

Barely distinguishable from other dots,
it's true, but quite uniquely placed.
And from my dark centre

I'd survey the beauty of the linescape
and wonder – would it be worthwhile
to roll myself towards the lemon stripe,

Centrally poised, and push my curves
against its edge, to get myself
a little extra attention?

But it's fine where I am.
I'll never make out what's going on
around me, and that's the joy of it.

The fact that I'm not a perfect circle
makes me more interesting in this world.
People will stare forever –

Even the most unemotional get excited.
So here I am, on the edge of animation,
a dream, a dance, a fantastic construction,

A child's adventure.
And nothing in this tawny sky
can get too close, or move too far away.

Throwing Out My Father's Dictionary

Words grow shoots in the bin
with the eggshells and rotting fruit.
It's years since the back fell off
to reveal paper edged with toffee-glue.
The preface is stained – a cloud rises
towards the use of the swung dash.

My father's signature is centre page,
arching letters underlined – I see him
rifling through his second language.

I retrieve it.
It smells of tarragon – my father's
dictionary, not quite finished with.

I have my own, weightier
with thousands of recent entries
arranged for me – like *chador*
and *sick building syndrome*
in the new wider pages.
I daren't inscribe my name.

Indian Cooking

The bottom of the pan was a palette –
paprika, cayenne, dhania
haldi, heaped like powder-paints.

Melted ghee made lakes, golden rivers.
The keema frying, my mother waited
for the fat to bubble to the surface.

Friends brought silver-leaf.
I dropped it on khir –
special rice pudding for parties.

I tasted the landscape, customs
of my father's country –
its fever on biting a chilli.

Presents from My Aunts in Pakistan

They sent me a salwar kameez
                    peacock-blue,
                            and another
            glistening like an orange split open,
embossed slippers, gold and black
                    points curling.
        Candy-striped glass bangles
                    snapped, drew blood.
        Like at school, fashions changed
                    in Pakistan –
the salwar bottoms were broad and stiff,
                    then narrow.
My aunts chose an apple-green sari,
        silver-bordered
                    for my teens.

I tried each satin-silken top –
        was alien in the sitting-room.
I could never be as lovely
                    as those clothes
        I longed
for denim and corduroy.
        My costume clung to me
                    and I was aflame,
I couldn't rise up out of its fire,
        half-English,
                    unlike Aunt Jamila.

I wanted my parents' camel-skin lamp –
    switching it on in my bedroom,
to consider the cruelty
            and the transformation
from camel to shade,
    marvel at the colours
            like stained glass.

My mother cherished her jewellery –
    Indian gold, dangling, filigree.
            But it was stolen from our car.
The presents were radiant in my wardrobe.
    My aunts requested cardigans
            from Marks and Spencers.

My salwar kameez
    didn't impress the schoolfriend
who sat on my bed, asked to see
    my weekend clothes.
But often I admired the mirror-work,
    tried to glimpse myself
            in the miniature
glass circles, recall the story
    how the three of us
            sailed to England.
Prickly heat had me screaming on the way.
    I ended up in a cot
in my English grandmother's dining-room,
    found myself alone,
            playing with a tin boat.

I pictured my birthplace
    from fifties' photographs.
            When I was older
there was conflict, a fractured land
    throbbing through newsprint.
Sometimes I saw Lahore –
            my aunts in shaded rooms,
screened from male visitors,
    sorting presents,
            wrapping them in tissue.

Or there were beggars, sweeper-girls
    and I was there –

           of no fixed nationality,
staring through fretwork
         at the Shalimar Gardens.

Arrival 1946

The boat docked in at Liverpool.
From the train Tariq stared
at an unbroken line of washing
from the North West to Euston.

These are strange people, he thought –
an Empire, and all this washing,
the underwear, the Englishman's garden.
It was Monday, and very sharp.

The Country at My Shoulder

There's a country at my shoulder,
growing larger – soon it will burst,
rivers will spill out, run down my chest.

My cousin Azam wants visitors to play
ludo with him all the time.
He learns English in a class of seventy.

And I must stand to attention
with the country at my shoulder.
There's an execution in the square –

The women's dupattas are wet with tears.
The offices have closed
for the white-hot afternoon.

But the women stone-breakers chip away
at boulders, dirt on their bright hems.
They await the men and the trucks.

I try to shake the dust from the country,
smooth it with my hands.
I watch Indian films –

Everyone is very unhappy,
or very happy,
dancing garlanded through parks.

I hear of bribery, family quarrels,
travellers' tales – the stars
are so low you think you can touch them.

Uncle Aqbar drives down the mountain
to arrange his daughter's marriage.
She's studying Christina Rossetti.

When the country bursts, we'll meet.
Uncle Kamil shot a tiger,
it hung over the wardrobe, its jaws

fixed in a roar – I wanted to hide
its head in a towel.
The country has become my body –

I can't break bits off.
The men go home in loose cotton clothes.
In the square there are those who beg –

and those who beg for mercy.
Azam passes the sweetshop,
names the sugar monuments Taj Mahal.

I water the country with English rain,
cover it with English words.
Soon it will burst, or fall like a meteor.

The Sari

Inside my mother
I peered through a glass porthole.
The world beyond was hot and brown.

They were all looking in on me –
Father, Grandmother,
the cook's boy, the sweeper-girl,
the bullock with the sharp
shoulderblades,
the local politicians.

My English grandmother
took a telescope
and gazed across continents.

All the people unravelled a sari.
It stretched from Lahore to Hyderabad,
wavered across the Arabian Sea,
shot through with stars,
fluttering with sparrows and quails.
They threaded it with roads,
undulations of land.

Eventually
they wrapped and wrapped me in it
whispering *Your body is your country.*

And If

If you could choose a country
to belong to –
perhaps you had one
snatched away,
once offered to you
like a legend
in a basket covered with a cloth –

and if the sun were a simple flare,
the streets beating out
the streets, and your breath
lost on the road
with the Yadavs, herding cattle,
then you could rest, absorb
it all in the cool of the hills,

but still you might peel back one face
to retrieve another
and another, down to the face that is
unbearable, so clear
so complex, hinting at nations,
castes and sub-castes
and you would touch it once –

and if this Eastern track were
a gusty English lane
where rain makes mirrors
in the holes,
a rat lies lifeless, sodden
as an old floorcloth,
you'd be untouchable – as one

defined by someone else –
one who cleans the toilets,
burns the dead.

The Wedding

I expected a quiet wedding
high above a lost city
a marriage to balance on my head

like a forest of sticks, a pot of water.
The ceremony tasted of nothing
had little colour – guests arrived

 stealthy as sandalwood smugglers.
When they opened their suitcases
England spilled out.

They scratched at my veil
like beggars on a car window.
I insisted my dowry was simple –

a smile, a shadow, a whisper,
my house an incredible structure
of stiffened rags and bamboo.

44

We travelled along roads with English
names, my bridegroom and I.
Our eyes changed colour

like traffic-lights, so they said.
The time was not ripe
for us to view each other.

We stared straight ahead as if
we could see through mountains
breathe life into new cities.

I wanted to marry a country
take up a river for a veil
sing in the Jinnah Gardens

hold up my dream, tricky
as a snake-charmer's snake.
Our thoughts half-submerged

like buffaloes under dark water
we turned and faced each other
with turbulence

and imprints like maps on our hands.

Houdini

It is not clear how he entered me
or why he always has to escape.
Maybe he's just proving to the crowds
he can still do it – he whispers
half-words which bloom in the dark
Ma ha ma ha.

Sometimes he feeds me cough medicine.
Or bathes his genitals in salt water.
Then heaves his body upwards
as if pressing against a lid.
At least he prefers me
to his underwater box, to the manacles

which clank on his moon-white skin.
I wonder what it is exactly
he sees within me?
He touches my insides as though
he'd sighted the first landplants –
I'm catching cloud between my fingers.

Tonight the wind whips through my stomach
over knots of trees and sharp rocks.
When he rushes out of me the crowd gasps –
and I implode from sheer emptiness.

Carrying My Wife

I carried my wife inside me –
like a cable car I pulled her
up the mountainside of our days.

I lifted her quite naturally
and I carried the floating,
prancing seahorse within her.

I took them both to the crossroads.
Stooping like St Christopher
I bore her – a slippery wave.

The hospital parted for us
strongly as the Red Sea.
I coaxed her through swings doors

which gusted to and fro
like our past and future.
She was sea-sick.

Sometimes she could hardly
remember who I was.
I only intended to leave her

for a moment in the bulrushes,
but she slept and slept,
hibernated like a star

gone to ground.
Then I carried her
to the ends of the Earth.

Man Impregnated

And I envied her the baby within,
tried to cultivate my own –
first with a cushion to simulate the bump.
Then I gained weight, soon became
a man impregnated with light and dark,
with violet, with the wrong food,
with small bottles of beer.
I soothed and patted my own bump,
felt the delicious fullness of it,
the groaning weight of it – until
at last I awoke with a glass abdomen.

I peered into it constantly,
saw in miniature my wife and myself,
upside down, slotted neatly into each other.
I had no morning sickness,
shortage of breath or indigestion,
but pressing against my ribcage
were the feelings I could scarcely own,
the rough creatures which fed off me.
I'd ask my wife to place her pregnant ear
to my stomach and listen to the trauma of the sea,
throwing us up as driftwood on the beach.

The International Stores

It was surely
the least international shop in the world.

I'd note the cheddar and the ham
supreme on the counter

like no-nonsense Anglo-Saxon parents.
But it was an emporium for tins –

splendid pyramids, more spectacular
than my grandmother's collection

stored in advance for World War Three.
The proud ranks of supplies created aisles

on the marbled chequered floor.
You could have got married here

in the sixties in the International Stores.
Your bridegroom would appear like a genie

out of a superior tin –
He would certainly be speaking English.

Mr Davenport, whiskery, and turning grey
through seriousness about merchandise,

would conduct the ceremony
from beside the weighing machine,

his hands like meticulous pink sausages
welcoming everyone, to the solemn

marriage of England to England,
the happy union of like minds.

The Other Family
(for Jackie Wills)

I stared at this other family
as if they were a clock
and I wanted to see the workings.
The only family a bit like us
in the town, in the whole universe.

A white parent, a dark parent
from Ceylon, darker even than my father,
as if he'd immersed himself
in the world's darkest substance.
And his wife was so pale,
like the underside of something.
I tried to envisage them
on the other side of a mirror –
their crushed sheets, midnight bedrooms.
I tried to hear their conversation.
I contemplated the children,
browner than I was, carrying
their English names like snowballs.
We hardly knew the parents –
I'd never seen inside their house.
But I was sure that as soon as
they touched each other
their hands would stick together.

Presents

Come closer.
It is Christmas morning.

The souls are opening their presents,
unpacking their empty boxes
in perfect harmony with the void.

Nothingness is the most sensible gift –
it doesn't clash with anything
and if you have some already
it isn't a problem to receive a little more.

The souls hold it shakily on a spoon
as if they are ravenous
as if they are about to eat.

This is the room reflected in the window.
Walk inside, explore it for yourself.
The fire is glacial crimson.

The walls are filmy, not like walls at all.
These are the most densely populated
living-rooms on earth.

But who lives in them? The souls
settle here in their multitudes,
visit the spines of weightless books,

the floating hands of clocks.
Sink into armchairs in the snow.
Lose interest in us, even

as they beat so fiercely
against our bolder rooms,
the glass of the world.

How the World Split in Two

Was it widthways or lengthways,
a quarrel with the equator?
Did the rawness of the inside sparkle?

Only this is true:
there was an arm on one side
and a hand on the other,
a thought on one side
and a hush on the other.

And a luminous tear
carried on the back of a beetle
went backwards and forwards
from one side to the other.

How a Long Way Off Rolled Itself Up

Once, there was a place called A Long Way Off –
it was too far away to contemplate.

All that was known
was that the grass was a strange texture,
the trees grew upside down, and the houses
appeared to have been turned inside out.

So people were unprepared
when A Long Way Off rolled itself up
and edged a little nearer, and kept on
moving, until it had ventured so close
you could smell it, and breathe in
its otherness.

People laughed uneasily. A Long Way Off
was close enough to singe their hair.

How the Children Were Born

Doctors and midwives were aghast.
There, embedded in each infant palm
was the barrel of a tiny gun.

Babies had always raged – but
could any child be born knowing,
and prepared for war?

Enmity was handed down
like an heirloom.
The guns grew with the babies,
poking like bone through the soft skin.

Half-and-Half

The thin line running from my navel downwards
meant, I thought, that I was half-and-half,

like the coffee my mother drank in restaurants.
That was sophisticated –

but to be half-and-half oneself? And one part
stemmed from a country that wasn't whole –

West and East Pakistan, on different sides
of the pendulous India, because powerful people

had carved up the world like the Sunday joint.
Pakistan belonged to the politicians, the priests.

And to my geography teacher who leapt across
ditches on field trips, and enlightened me

briskly as to where I was born.
Discomfited, I put the pin on the map.

Rural Scene

The luminous Norfolk skies,
the tractors, the gunshots,
the still ponds, the darting rabbits,
cow parsley by the field gates –

all are re-imagining themselves
because Tariq walks in his village,
part of the scene, yet conspicuous,
as if he is walking a tiger.

IMTIAZ DHARKER

Imtiaz Dharker's cultural experience spans three countries. Born in 1954 in Lahore, Pakistan, she grew up a Muslim Calvinist in a Lahori household in Glasgow, later eloping with a Hindu Indian to live in Bombay. She now lives between Mumbai (where she makes documentary films), London and Wales. It is from this life of transitions that she draws her main themes: childhood, exile, journeying, home, displacement, religious strife and terror. 'I knew I didn't belong in one place,' she has said, 'but I began to feel strongly that this wasn't a bad thing...My real country and culture is movement, transition, crossing over.'

She is also an accomplished artist (pictured above at one of her exhibitions). Her first collection *Purdah* was published in India in 1989, and she has since published three books in Britain with Bloodaxe, all including her own drawings: *Postcards from god* [including *Purdah*] (1997), *I speak for the devil* (2001) and *The terrorist at my table* (2006). The selection of poems here is from all her books.

In *Purdah*, she is a traveller between cultures, while in *Postcards from god*, she imagines an anguished god surveying a world stricken by fundamentalism. In *I speak for the devil*, the woman's body is a territory, a thing that is possessed, owned by herself or by another. Her sequence *They'll say, 'She must be from another country'* traces a journey, starting with a striptease where the claims of nationality, religion and gender are cast off, to allow an exploration of new territories, the spaces *between* countries, cultures and religions.

The title-sequence speaks for the devil in acknowledging that in many societies women are respected, or listened to, only when they are carrying someone else inside their bodies – a child; a devil. For some, to be "possessed" is to be set free.

The terrorist at my table asks crucial questions about how we live now – working, travelling, eating, listening to the news, preparing for attack. What do any of us know about the person who shares this street, this house, this table, this body? When life is in the hands of a fellow-traveller, a neighbour, a lover, son or daughter, how does the world shift and reform itself around our doubt, our belief?

SOME RESPONSES TO IMTIAZ DHARKER'S WORK:

'In *Purdah* she memorialises the betweenness of a traveller between cultures, exploring the dilemmas of negotiation among countries, lovers, children. *Postcards from god* meditates upon disquietudes in the poet's chosen society: its sudden acts of violence, its feuds and insanities, forcing her into a permanent wakefulness that fits her eyes with glass lids. If the poems collected in *Purdah* are windows shuttered upon a private world, those gathered into *Postcards from god* are doorways leading out into the lanes and shanties where strangers huddle, bereft of the tender grace of attention.

'The poems are amplified by powerful black and white drawings by the author. The line is Imtiaz Dharker's sole weapon in a zone of assault which stretches over the Indian subcontinent's bloody history, the shifting dynamics of personal relationships and the torment of an individual caught between two cultures, divergent world-views' – RANJIT HOSKOTE, *The Times of India*.

'Hers is a strong, concerned, economical poetry, in which political activity, homesickness, urban violence, religious anomalies, are raised in an unobtrusive domestic setting, all the more effectively for their coolness of treatment' – ALAN ROSS, *London Magazine*.

'Here is no glib internationalism or modish multiculturalism... Displacement here no longer spells exile; it means an exhilarating sense of life at the interstices. There is an exultant celebration of a self that strips off layers of superfluous identity with grace and abandon, only to discover that it has not diminished, but grown larger, generous, more inclusive' – ARUNDHATHI SUBRAMANIAM, *Poetry International*.

INTERVIEWS: **Menka Shivdasani:** extract from interview in *Just Between Us: Women Speak About Their Writing*, ed. Ammu Joseph, Vasanth Kannabiran, Ritu Menon, Gouri Salvi & Volga (Women Unlimited, Delhi, 2004); **Alexandra Hamlyn:** extract from interview in *Kee Magazine*, 18 (Winter 2005), Hong Kong.

from Interview with Imtiaz Dharker
by MENKA SHIVDASANI

MS: You were born in Pakistan, grew up in Glasgow and now divide your time between Mumbai and London. What impact have these cultural transitions had on your writing? Have you ever felt you were the "outsider" looking in?

ID: As I say in the poem, 'Front door', there was one country inside the house and one outside, but I didn't see that as a difficulty. I could easily slip from one to the other, the way children slip from one language to another if they are bilingual. Growing up in Glasgow, in a way I was an outsider. In the outside world I was a young girl getting an education, doing anything that she wanted to – but there were some limitations. I would sit in libraries, but was not allowed to go out with friends in the evening.

MS: What was your childhood like, growing up in Scotland? What kind of influence did Pakistan have on your lifestyle?

ID: I was one year old when I left Pakistan, so except as an idea it wasn't really there. It was just a background for me. Glasgow was tough, but it was a good place to grow up in. There were Sunday picnics in Loch Lomond and the Campsie Fells – it was very beautiful. We were not overly religious. There was belief but it wasn't pushed down my throat.

MS: When did you first go back to Pakistan?

ID: When I was 13. I remember everything seemed so amazingly lush. I knew I had finally come to a landscape with which I was comfortable. I'd never been happy getting up on cold winter mornings and going to school. It seemed incredible, there was fruit lying on the road, piles of oranges and watermelons. Even in Glasgow, my mother would come back with some amazingly exotic fruit, things like watermelon and tangerines. Those were very special parts of a life I knew had existed in the past, somewhere, maybe some residual collective memory of paradise gardens, because she always turned up with these things that were difficult to find – pomegranates, aubergines. They were very exotic at that time. So when I came across this lush landscape, all those fields of maize and fruit, it was like a dream come true. I knew it had always been there.

MS: Did the difference in cultures create any problems?

ID: My family cut me off when I married an Indian Hindu, but his mother was fine...She had a reception for us and said it wasn't that she wanted the ritual, but that she wanted to show the world she was happy. But one day I found myself in front of a Ganpati [elephant-headed Hindu deity] doing a *puja* [act of showing reverence] and ringing a bell. I suddenly thought, 'I just can't do this. Given my background I just can't do it.' I come from a background where God must be disembodied, a religion of The Book, and I had not realised till then how deeply ingrained this was.

It was only much later, when my daughter, Ayesha, was born, and she began to enjoy all the religions, the festivals, Ganpati, that I began to see it as a joyous expression, another way of building equations with God, and not as a fraught religious divide. I began to open up to the idea that if it could give joy, it was a route...

For many, many years I've been saying Islam is a great religion, I can see that everything in the religion is right, but it is being badly, badly misused by men. As I think Hinduism and Christianity have been misused for centuries to suppress women. The ones interpreting the religions are all men; it is a very simple way of maintaining the status quo, the power equations. So I wouldn't say my acceptance was because I was rejecting Islam – in fact, I was opening up to other routes. And all that time I was writing, reading quietly.

MS: Quietly?

ID: It was all about personal feelings and again, there's this business of not wanting to let anyone know how you feel. It wasn't about love, romance or men, but I was always very private and didn't want anyone to know. I was also reading a lot – in fact, the first present I gave Anil was Dom Moraes' *John Nobody*. And he gave me Eliot's work. Then there was Gerard Manley Hopkins. Hopkins was a great revelation, the way he constructed his words, the anti-form of what he was doing. He was a revolutionary, the way he was handling rhyme and rhythm, and there was a lovely spin to it.

MS: Were there any women writers who influenced you?

ID: Not at that time. Much later, Carol Ann Duffy, Jo Shapcott, Fleur Adcock, Selima Hill, lovely writer. There was very little in terms of women's writing being heard of or seen in schools.

MS: Do you find your drawings are linked to your poems in any way?

ID: They are. At first I tried to keep them separate. In fact, when my first book was being published, I spoke to Nissim Ezekiel and said, there are drawings too and he said, 'Keep them apart, don't mix the two.' And it was probably good advice at that time, but slowly I found I just couldn't keep the drawings and poems separate because they amplified each other. I finally decided I would not only *not* try to separate them, but I would work them together.

MS: Your third book, *I speak for the devil*, seems to follow as a natural progression from *Postcards from god*. Had you planned it this way or did you find there was a natural pattern, some common themes that hold the body of your work together?

ID: I think the base was how to handle social equations and how to make sense of what happens in the world. When I began to question the whole idea of god and the power of god, what god's role and a human being's role is, when I began to look at the chaos of the world, I started to ask, how on earth could this happen? I presumptuously cast God as a bewildered person in *Postcards from god*, a person who could not understand the routes the world had taken.

A lot of the early writing was coming to grips with images. First of all that seductive image of *Purdah* – as a graphic it's beautiful, with all the emphasis on the eyes and everything else a black frame, a beautiful image; and then working around it as an idea, seeing it as oppression. The whole first lot of writing really had to do with what set of images belonged to me, what I could lay claim to. In that context, what do I believe about the whole baggage of beliefs that go with a culture, a religion?

Purdah was beginning to deal with territory, borderlines, the whole question of where you divide people. The first set of drawings was to do with that, with spaces between the bodies. What's happened is a progression from an inward-looking, internalising of those images to an outward one, the impact of the world being felt every day. I can't write without being very affected by the very strange things happening in the world. I find it so inconceivable sometimes ...the way politicians behave, the way the world bites its own tail. The way the lines blur between who is good and bad, what is good and bad, the way the saviour turns out to be Satan...

MS: One of the major themes of your poetry is the oppression of women, the observation that a woman's body is often a territory, a thing that is owned by another, respected only when they are carrying someone inside their bodies – a child, or a spirit, for instance...

ID: Society pushes women; even if they pretend you can speak, they don't want to hear. By society I mean a society of men, really, and a lot women go along. In one of my poems, 'The djinn in Auntie', freedom to the woman is the *djinn* inside her, the voice that people can't control. And she wants to keep that voice, that is her freedom.

57

Imtiaz Dharker's Art: Interview
by ALEXANDRA HAMLYN

AH: How would you respond to yourself being labelled as a political artist – what does this mean to you?

ID: My work is not political in the sense of being propagandist or having a political agenda. But it is certainly affected by what is happening in the world. It does have a political context. Even when Turner painted skies and cityscapes, or Wordsworth wrote about daffodils, it was within the context of industrialisation, and their views on it. When I draw or write, the images I use have to come out of my everyday environment. But remember that the environment for all of us has changed. The television set, for example, is a lodger in the living-room. The woman onscreen becomes my neighbour. News images are as much part of the landscape as the street or field outside the window. If I pretend they aren't there, it would be like blinding one of my eyes.

AH: Your technique and style question our sense of identity through expressive metaphor, how do you feel your response to gender and communal conflicts has encouraged your artistic expression? How is this different from your poetic expression?

ID: For me, writing a poem and drawing are like crossing the same terrain by different forms of transport. They explore different aspects of an image. I use the human face in various ways. I hope these drawings work, at the simplest level, as image, composition, an arrangement of lines. Beyond that, I am trying to look at the face not as a portrait but as an unfolding landscape; and then come to the inner landscape, the hidden self, the fragmented self, the mask, the veil, the cloth unfolding, cloth as concealer and revealer, cloth as an instrument of seduction, cloth as a threat.

AH: Why have you chosen to present your work in such an alluring way through stark contrast in black and white, yet with a softness to your technique – this is quite contradictory, don't you think?

ID: There's no contradiction. The drawings are not trying to do just one thing. I've tried to suggest the hidden face, and make the cloth live and ambiguous. It can seduce, it can be misconstrued, it can threaten. The black and white is a function of my medium: pen and ink on paper. To me, this is not so much stark as pure. If there is austerity, it comes from an attempt to strip away what isn't essential. Again, if there is softness it is to do with the medium.

Blessing

The skin cracks like a pod.
There never is enough water.

Imagine the drip of it,
the small splash, echo
in a tin mug,
the voice of a kindly god.

Sometimes, the sudden rush
of fortune. The municipal pipe bursts,
silver crashes to the ground
and the flow has found
a roar of tongues. From the huts,
a congregation: every man woman
child for streets around
butts in, with pots,
brass, copper, aluminium,
plastic buckets,
frantic hands,

and naked children
screaming in the liquid sun,
their highlights polished to perfection,
flashing light,
as the blessing sings
over their small bones.

Purdah I

One day they said
she was old enough to learn some shame.
She found it came quite naturally.

Purdah is a kind of safety.
The body finds a place to hide.
The cloth fans out against the skin
much like the earth that falls
on coffins after they put the dead men in.

People she has known
stand up, sit down as they have always done.
But they make different angles
in the light, their eyes aslant,
a little sly.

She half-remembers things
from someone else's life,
perhaps from yours, or mine –
carefully carrying what we do not own:
between the thighs, a sense of sin.

We sit still, letting the cloth grow
a little closer to our skin.
A light filters inward
through our bodies' walls.
Voices speak inside us,
echoing in the spaces we have just left.

She stands outside herself,
sometimes in all four corners of a room.
Wherever she goes, she is always
inching past herself,
as if she were a clod of earth
and the roots as well,
scratching for a hold
between the first and second rib.

Passing constantly out of her own hands
into the corner of someone else's eyes...
while doors keep opening
inward and again
inward.

Postcards from god I

Yes, I do feel like a visitor,
a tourist in this world
that I once made.
I rarely talk,
except to ask the way,

distrusting my interpreters,
tired out by the babble
of what they do not say.
I walk around through battered streets,
distinctly lost,
looking for landmarks
from another, promised past.

Here, in this strange place,
in a disjointed time,
I am nothing but a space
that someone has to fill.
Images invade me.
Picture postcards overlap my empty face,
demanding to be stamped and sent.

'Dear...'

Who am I speaking to?
I think I may have misplaced the address,
but still, I feel the need
to write to you;
not so much for your sake
as for mine,

to raise these barricades
against my fear:
Postcards from god.
Proof that I was here.

Living Space

There are just not enough
straight lines. That
is the problem.
Nothing is flat
or parallel. Beams
balance crookedly on supports
thrust off the vertical.
Nails clutch at open seams.
The whole structure leans dangerously
towards the miraculous.

Into this rough frame,
someone has squeezed
a living space

and even dared to place
these eggs in a wire basket,
fragile curves of white
hung out over the dark edge
of a slanted universe,
gathering the light
into themselves,
as if they were
the bright, thin walls of faith.

Minority

I was born a foreigner.
I carried on from there
to become a foreigner everywhere
I went, even in the place
planted with my relatives,
six-foot tubers sprouting roots,
their fingers and faces pushing up
new shoots of maize and sugar cane.

All kinds of places and groups
of people who have an admirable
history would, almost certainly,
distance themselves from me.

I don't fit,
like a clumsily translated poem;

like food cooked in milk of coconut
where you expected ghee or cream,
the unexpected aftertaste
of cardamom or neem.

There's always that point where
the language flips

into an unfamiliar taste;
where words tumble over
a cunning tripwire on the tongue;
where the frame slips,
the reception of an image
not quite tuned, ghost-outlined,
that signals, in their midst,
an alien.

And so I scratch, scratch
through the night, at this
growing scab of black on white.
Everyone has the right
to infiltrate a piece of paper.
A page doesn't fight back.
And, who knows, these lines
may scratch their way
into your head –
through all the chatter of community,
family, clattering spoons,
children being fed –
immigrate into your bed,
squat in your home,
and in a corner, eat your bread,

until, one day, you meet
the stranger sidling down your street,
realise you know the face
simplified to bone,
look into its outcast eyes
and recognise it as your own.

The Name of god

I was washing my daughter's hair.
That was when they started
pounding at the door
banging with their sticks, and swords.
Then the fire
spread across the floor.

We ran out through the back,
her hair still wet and full of soap,
past the neighbourhood boys
with hatchets, hacking
out the name of god.

And running, we too breathed the name.
But on our tongues
it did not sound the same.

It had the sound
of children whispering,
water lapping in a pot,
the still flame of an oil-lamp.

The name of god
in my mouth
had a taste I soon forgot.

I think it was the taste
of home.

Honour killing

At last I'm taking off this coat,
    this black coat of a country
    that I swore for years was mine,
    that I wore more out of habit
    than design.
    Born wearing it,
    I believed I had no choice.

I'm taking off this veil,
    this black veil of a faith
    that made me faithless
    to myself,
    that tied my mouth,
    gave my god a devil's face,
    and muffled my own voice.

I'm taking off these silks,
    these lacy things
    that feed dictator dreams,
    the mangalsutra and the rings
    rattling in a tin cup of needs
    that beggared me.

I'm taking off this skin,
    and then the face, the flesh,
    the womb.

Let's see
    what I am in here
    when I squeeze past
    the easy cage of bone.

Let's see
    what I am out here,
    making, crafting,
    plotting
    at my new geography.

Front door

Wherever I have lived,
walking out of the front door
every morning
means crossing over
to a foreign country.

One language inside the house,
another out.
The food and clothes
and customs change.
The fingers on my hand turn
into forks.

I call it adaptation
when my tongue switches
from one grammar to another,
but the truth is I'm addicted now,

high on the rush
of daily displacement,
speeding to a different time zone,
heading into altered weather,
landing as another person.

Don't think I haven't noticed
you're on the same trip too.

They'll say, 'She must be from another country'

When I can't comprehend
why they're burning books
or slashing paintings,
when they can't bear to look
at god's own nakedness,
when they ban the film
and gut the seats to stop the play
and I ask why
they just smile and say,
'She must be
from another country.'

When I speak on the phone
and the vowel sounds are off
when the consonants are hard
and they should be soft,
they'll catch on at once
they'll pin it down
they'll explain it right away
to their own satisfaction,
they'll cluck their tongues
and say,
'She must be
from another country.'

When my mouth goes up
instead of down,
when I wear a tablecloth
to go to town,
when they suspect I'm black

or hear I'm gay
they won't be surprised,
they'll purse their lips
and say,
'She must be
from another country.'

When I eat up the olives
and spit out the pits
when I yawn at the opera
in the tragic bits
when I pee in the vineyard
as if it were Bombay,
flaunting my bare ass
covering my face
laughing through my hands
they'll turn away,
shake their heads quite sadly,
'She doesn't know any better,'
they'll say,
'She must be
from another country.'

Maybe there is a country
where all of us live,
all of us freaks
who aren't able to give
our loyalty to fat old fools,
the crooks and thugs
who wear the uniform
that gives them the right
to wave a flag,
puff out their chests,
put their feet on our necks,
and break their own rules.

But from where we are
it doesn't look like a country,
it's more like the cracks
that grow between borders
behind their backs.
That's where I live.
And I'll be happy to say,
'I never learned your customs.

I don't remember your language
or know your ways.
I must be
from another country.'

This room

This room is breaking out
of itself, cracking through
its own walls
in search of space, light,
empty air.

The bed is lifting out of
its nightmares.
From dark corners, chairs
are rising up to crash through clouds.

This is the time and place
to be alive:
when the daily furniture of our lives
stirs, when the improbable arrives.
Pots and pans bang together
in celebration, clang
past the crowd of garlic, onions, spices,
fly by the ceiling fan.
No one is looking for the door.

In all this excitement
I'm wondering where
I've left my feet, and why

my hands are outside, clapping.

Platform

On the platform opposite
three men and one woman
are reading newspapers,

six people are speaking into phones,
or listening. One is sitting on a tin
case marked 'Fragile'.
A boy yawns, then
looks at the girl wearing green boots.

The board shuffles
through its pack of numbers.
A poster offers Escape Routes.
Trains come and go.

Now only four on phones.
Where did that man
go, carrying his fragile cargo?
Easy to lose count.
Some leave in time. Some stay.

The terrorist at my table

I slice sentences to turn them into
onions. On this chopping board, they
seem more organised,
as if with a little effort
I could begin
to understand their shape.

At my back, the news is the same
as usual. A train
blown up, hostages taken.
Outside, in Pollokshields, the rain.

I go upstairs, come down.
I go to the kitchen.
When things are in their place,
they look less difficult.
I cut and chop. I don't need to see,
through onion tears,
my own hand power the knife.

Here is the food. I put it on the table.
The tablecloth is fine cutwork,

sent from home. Beneath it, Gaza
is a spreading watermark.

Here are the facts, fine
as onion rings.
The same ones can come chopped
or sliced.

Shoes, kitchens, onions can be left
behind, but at a price.
Knowledge is something you can choose
to give away,
but giving and taking leave a stain.

Who gave the gift of Palestine?

Cut this. Chop this,
this delicate thing
haloed in onion skin.

Your generosity turns my hands
to knives,
the tablecloth to fire.

Outside, on the face of Jerusalem,
I feel the rain.

Campsie Fells

What did we look like?
A band of gypsies
set free out of solid homes
for one Sunday morning,
catapulted into the countryside,
a caravan.
All the families, Auntie Ameena,
Uncle Ramzan, a variety of children
in flowered frocks and wide shalwars,
clothes that responded to the wind.

What were we like, on that
Scottish field, up in the hills,
navigating the cow-pats,
paddling in sweet streams?

The children made daisy chains.
Azaan
shone a buttercup beneath our chins
to check if we loved butter.

And when the picnic was opened out,
the competition began, between
the families.
Who brought boiled eggs and sandwiches,
who made kebabs and tikkas with chutney.
The thermos flasks of tea,
all made up with sugar and with milk.

My mother settled like a queen,
a sculpture, took possession of that field,
spread all her goods around her.

The green sharpened.
The sun always blazed,
The long evenings never grew cold.

The Aunties began to speak
about old films, *Alvida, Alvida*
sang bits of songs
that always sounded sad,
Tum bhi kho gaye, hum bhi kho gaye.
Lines of remembered poems
made Uncle Asif cry.
Azaan asked, 'If you mind so much,
why don't you go back?'

Uncle Asif, wiping his eyes, replied,
'Our families are scattered. My brothers
and their wives are here. The village has changed.
My uncles have moved to town.
I'm not sure if anyone knows us any more.
And would you go get Zenab
out of the cow-shit and wash your hands
before you touch those chips?'

Afterwards we washed the cups.
Our names splashed in the stream,
no questions asked.

Before I

This is what was happening
before the planes came in.
She woke early,

switched on the songs,
fetched milk and put it on to heat.
Bare feet slapped across the floor.

She shook the children awake,
her voice a little hoarse
from sleep.

She was thinking about
what she would pack
for them to eat

at school, something
cooling in the heat.
And now, the water.

The water spilling
out of a steel glass.

All this happened
before.

˄ These are the times we live in I

You hand over your passport. He
looks at your face and starts
reading you backwards from the last page.

You could be offended,
but in the end, you decide
it makes as much sense
as anything else,
given the times we live in.

You shrink to the size
of the book in his hand.
You can see his mind working:
Keep an eye on that name.
It contains a Z, and it just moved house.
The birthmark shifted recently
to another arm or leg.
Nothing is quite the same
as it should be.
But what do you expect?
It's a sign of the times we live in.

In front of you,
he flicks to the photograph,
and looks at you suspiciously.

That's when you really have to laugh.
While you were flying,
up in the air
they changed your chin
and redid your hair.
They scrubbed out your mouth
and rubbed out your eyes.
They made you over completely.

And all that's left is his look of surprise,
because you don't match your photograph.
Even that is coming apart.

The pieces are there
but they missed out your heart.

Half your face splits away,
drifts on to the page of a newspaper
that's dated today.

It rustles as it lands.

How to cut a pomegranate

'Never,' said my father,
'Never cut a pomegranate
through the heart. It will weep blood.
Treat it delicately, with respect.

Just slit the upper skin across four quarters.
This is a magic fruit,
so when you split it open, be prepared
for the jewels of the world to tumble out,
more precious than garnets,
more lustrous than rubies,
lit as if from inside.
Each jewel contains a living seed.
Separate one crystal.
Hold it up to catch the light.
Inside is a whole universe.
No common jewel can give you this.'

Afterwards, I tried to make necklaces
of pomegranate seeds.
The juice spurted out, bright crimson,
and stained my fingers, then my mouth.

I didn't mind. The juice tasted of gardens
I had never seen, voluptuous
with myrtle, lemon, jasmine,
and alive with parrots' wings.

The pomegranate reminded me
that somewhere I had another home.

JACKIE KAY

Jackie Kay was an adopted child of Scottish/Nigerian descent brought up by white parents. With humour and emotional directness, her poetry explores gender, sexuality, identity, racism and cultural difference as well as love and music. She has published four collections of poetry with Bloodaxe. All her books draw on people's lives, including her own, in a search for personal identity, fictionalising autobiography and telling other people's stories through personae or dramatic mono-logues. The title of her short story collection, *Why Don't You Stop Talking* (Picador, 2002), could almost be a comment on her poems, in which everyone talks as if their lives depended upon speaking up and speaking out; it is through talking her characters into being that Jackie Kay creates her own sense of self through her poems, which are conversational in tone but with jazz-inflected rhythms.

Her other books include *Trumpet* (Picador, 1998), a novel inspired by the life of musician Billy Tipton, which tells the story of Scottish jazz trumpeter Joss Moody, who lived her life disguised as a man. A half-hour reading by Jackie Kay is included on the cassette *The Poetry Quartets: 1* (The British Council/Bloodaxe Books, 1998).

Born in 1961 in Edinburgh, Jackie Kay grew up in Glasgow, studying at the Royal Scottish Academy of Music and Drama and at Stirling University. She is a freelance writer who has won wide acclaim and received many awards for her poetry, fiction, drama and children's books. She lives in Manchester with her son.

The title-sequence of her first collection, *The Adoption Papers*

(1991), written in three voices, tells the story of a black girl's adoption by a white Glaswegian couple – a much loved daughter growing up in a communist household but experiencing racism at school. Other poems in the book focus on love, gay relationships, prejudice and the loss of loved ones to AIDS.

Other Lovers (1993) shows her delving further into history and culture, exploring the role and power of language as well as the qualities of love in a variety of relationships, rooted in the past or present. The poems move from the familiar to the extraordinary, including a sequence on Blues singer Bessie Smith.

The main themes of *Off Colour* (1998) are sickness, health and disease, expressed through personal experience and metaphor. These poems examine not just the sick body, but the sick mind, the sick society, the sickness of racism and prejudice. 'Hottentot Venus' is about Saartjie Bartmaan, a 19th-century African woman exhibited at carnivals (also the subject of a poem by Elizabeth Alexander, written around the same time: see page 15). In 'Pride', written after an encounter with a mysterious Nigerian on a train, Jackie Kay imagines meeting her birth father for the first time, unaware within a few years the actual event will occur, as she recalls in a group of poems in *Life Mask* (2005) which include 'Things Fall Apart'.

Life Mask focuses on love, loss, and mistaken and secret identity. The poems reveal how we hide from each other and from ourselves, how appearances are deceptive and how many faces it takes to make even the one self. They peel back all the selves to go closer to the bone, refusing to flinch at all the faces of love, whose truth is often hooded or disguised and honesty itself can be a kind of mask.

RUTH PADEL ON JACKIE KAY'S WORK:

'Disease is her metaphor for social cruelty, especially racism...Kay has always linked her poems strongly. The linking principle in *Off Colour* is identity, bizarrely intertwined with dentistry...witty, risky, lyrical, teasing; rich, strong, socially questioning. Cleverness at the service of feeling...putting vulnerability, both emotional and physical, squarely on the line...' [Reviewing *Off Colour* in *The Independent*.]

'This poet's history – a black child adopted and reared in Scotland – and the personae that have shone from her previous books in many genres since her first collection, *The Adoption Papers*, make reforging this particular identity an unusually complex matter. In different forms, tones and voices, these poems flicker fascinatingly between oppositions...The poems explore authenticity, allegiance, origins and memory through multiple masks.' [Reviewing *Life Mask*.]

Interview with Jackie Kay *by* LAURA SEVERIN

LS: What poetic traditions do you see yourself a part of? You write in your novel, *Trumpet*, about making, at least partially, your own ancestry; who are your ancestors?

JK: I see myself as coming out of two, quite distinct traditions. On the one hand, there's the tradition of Scottish poetry itself – Burns, Burns Suppers, and that kind of a tradition in Scotland, where you would get to hear poetry being read and performed out loud. At events like that, you actually have, for instance, an address to the haggis, where somebody recites a poem to the haggis, or an address to the lassies. I used to go to those a lot as a child, Burns Suppers, every single year, sometimes three different Burns Suppers a year. They made a huge impression on me. I loved it that poetry could be performed, that poetry could be dramatic. I really do see myself as being part of a tradition that wants to see the drama that is in poetry, through its poetic voices. So that is one kind of tradition. On the other hand, I also am very interested, and always have been, in music. I see that my poetry is influenced by jazz and blues, as well as by Celtic folk songs and music. Lots of the rhythms and the repetitions that are in my poetry are closely related to music and come out of musical tradition. So, it's two, quite distinct, but, to me, connected traditions.

LS: Can you say more about how jazz and blues have influenced your poetry?

JK: Without the jazz and blues traditions, my poetry wouldn't be the same. It's consciously and also unconsciously influenced by jazz and blues – how much is conscious and how much is unconscious I don't actually know, because one never knows these things. It's not an exact science. I did listen to jazz and blues a lot when I was growing up and I loved it instinctively – loved it as if it was already part of me, as if it already belonged to me. It already seemed my music even as a small child of ten or eleven when everybody else was listening to Donny Osmond and David Cassidy or the Bay City Rollers. Then I was listening to Duke Ellington, Bessie Smith, Count Basie and Billie Holiday – these are the people that I really love. Charlie Parker. I love that business of sitting and counting the beats, listening to the beats and tapping my foot like my dad. I was very fortunate that I had a dad who loved jazz and blues. He played it a lot when he was home. It was also fortunate that I had

a best friend who loved jazz and blues. We used to mimic Pearl
Bailey. We had this album of Pearl Bailey and she'd sing 'Tired of
the life I lead, tired of the Blues I be'. So we'd do these songs. We'd
put the record on and then one of us would get up and pretend to
be Bailey. We spent hours doing that and it was really fantastic. I
think that a lot of that actual metre, the 12/4 bar beat of the blues,
and then the looser jazz forms, in the later jazz songs, went into
my writing. Some of my poems have got that quite strict 12/4 blues
kind of a metre. Others have got the other sort of jazz flow. It pro-
vides fuel, allows me to really take off on certain riffs. I definitely
think that one can trace the music in my work. So yes, I definitely
think it's a great influence.

LS: Do you ever have specific songs in mind when you write your
poems, like Stevie Smith did, for instance?

JK: No, I never do that because I like the reader to have freedom.
That would be too much directing my reader... When I write, I
actually think about it consciously, about creating a space so that
readers can come in with their life, their experiences, their disappoint-
ments, and their loves. I want it to be like the call and response of
the blues. So, I'm happiest if a reader comes up to me and says, 'Oh
that bit meant so much to me because that was exactly like such and
such that happened in my life.' That makes me happier than anything
else as a writer. You as writer call and the reader responds.

LS: What contemporary poets form your poetic community? That
is, which poets do you identify with, even if you don't personally
know them?

JK: Well, I identify with Liz Lochhead. She was one of the first
poets that I ever heard. I think that certain people are flame carriers
for a whole lot of people to come after them. I would say that with-
out Liz Lochhead I wouldn't exist. Lochhead was one of the first
women poets that made it possible to speak in her own voice, which
was a Scottish voice. That was very different, very original, when
she first started writing. I went to hear her when I was a schoolgirl,
16 years old. It was the same with Tom Leonard, another Scottish
poet, who has been around for a long time. I got very excited when
I first heard both of them.
    Then, there is an American group of poets that really influenced
me, Audre Lorde being one of them, as well as Nikki Giovanni and
Ntozake Shange. When I first heard and read all of their work, I
felt very excited. They were able to explore being a woman and
being what a woman meant, in Audre Lorde's case being a black

lesbian and a poet. At that time, I didn't know anybody existed that was like me at all. They were able to do that through their poetry. I suppose I didn't see anyone who was a reflection of me because there weren't very many black poets writing then in this country. I got the Scottishness from the Scottish poets and the blackness from the American poets, largely. As a result, I have never felt myself to be part of one distinct tradition because, I suppose, my identity is quite complex. I get what I can from where I can get it. I don't feel that I have a single hero therefore, in the way that some poets do.

LS: Yes, as an American, your poetry has always seemed familiar, perhaps because of the influences of those African-American women writers.

JK: Well, that's definitely true, and, at one stage, these writers influenced me much more than the Scottish poets. You go through various trying on of clothes as far as identity is concerned, rejecting some things about yourself and accepting others. So, at one stage, I felt annoyed with being Scottish and rejected everything to do with being Scottish. I just wanted to embrace being black because for so many years I hadn't done that. So, at one stage, that was who I was reading, African-American writers, everybody from poets to novelists – Gayle Jones, Gloria Naylor, Maya Angelou, Toni Morrison. These writers influenced me a lot. I didn't want to write like them, that's another thing that's important when you think about influence. Influence doesn't necessarily mean that you're going to try and create a similar thing; it just means that you broaden your perspective and see what's possible.

LS: How has your poetry changed over the years?

JK: When I was a kid, I wrote these polemical poems about things that I disagreed with or things that I felt very angry about; you know, poverty and apartheid and war and greed and rich people being rich and poor people being poor. I was a little child who would write these very angry poems about the world. Very early on I had a strong sense of social justice, right and wrong. I think that's one of the things that children today are missing because we live in a society that doesn't seem concerned about the state of the world. That, to me, is horrifying. I keep trying to give my son a sense of social consciousness about the world. It's difficult to do now. I describe my early poems as being those morbid, depressed teenage sort of poems, terrible mushroom-taking kinds of poems. Then they came out of that. I remember sending my poems off when they were very polemical, to places like *Spare Rib*, and getting letters back saying that they were very good but there wasn't enough *me* in them. It was too much *issue* and not enough *me*. So then I went to the other end of the extreme and wrote all these poems that were about me and I found that when I did start to write personally, quite personally, that I didn't like them either. So then, I finally cracked it and found a way that was writing about myself but also not writing myself.

When I started to write *The Adoption Papers*, I felt as if I'd really become a poet. I felt as if all the other stuff beforehand was just the preparation. I felt, yes, that I could write poetry that was informed by my life but was also imaginary. I could use both; I could combine the two, which is still the thing that I find the most interesting to do – to take a bit of the real and a bit of the imaginary, a bit of the familiar and a bit of the strange, and blend those things together in some sort of way.

LS: Yes, I love that combination in your work.

JK: Once I'd started to do that with myself, I found I could create these other personas, and I moved on to dramatic monologues, which are represented in the second half of *The Adoption Papers* and then in *Other Lovers*. But now I've moved away from writing dramatic monologues in poetry... I'm more interested now in try-ing to find a way of returning to lyric poetry – but with a lot of drama...intimate and lyrical and personal but also dramatic, without having to create the voices of characters.

Excerpt from an interview published on the *FreeVerse* website drawing on conversations in Manchester and Raleigh, NC (USA) from September 2001 to February 2002. Copyright © 2002 by FreeVerse. For the full text, see: go to http://english.chass.ncsu.edu/freeverse/Archives/Spring_2002/Interviews/interviews.htm

Jackie Kay WRITES...

A strange thing happens when you have to write or talk about your own work: it becomes like the work of somebody else and you try to think of something to say after the event. The 'event' which really matters is the writing and what you say afterwards is as false as hindsight. We are our own unreliable narrators. Take this with a pinch of salt.

I think I will always be interested in identity, how fluid it is, how people can invent themselves, how it can never be fixed or frozen. In *The Adoption Papers*, I took my own life as a subject and fictionalised it. I was adopted and brought up in Scotland. The 'Somebody Else' in another poem here is the other person I could possibly have been. Fate is mixed up with identity. My original birth father was Nigerian: 'Pride' takes my face as a kind of a map back to the imaginary Nigeria.

I like mixing fact with fiction and trying to illuminate the border country that exists between them. Being black and Scottish, I've often been asked where I'm from. 'In my country' is a mixture of many experiences. 'Twelve Bar Bessie' was also inspired by a real incident when Bessie Smith fought off the Ku Klux Klan single-handedly. I've loved Bessie Smith's raunchy blues since I was a girl, and wrote about her in *Bessie*. I like the way that jazz too is fluid. I've written a novel, *Trumpet*, about a jazz trumpeter who lives his life as a man but is discovered to be a woman after death. From blues narratives on, I've always been interested in the way music tells the story of identity.

From *New Blood*, ed. Neil Astley (Bloodaxe Books, 1999).

from The Adoption Papers
Chapter 3: The Waiting Lists

The first agency we went to
didn't want us on their lists,
we didn't live close enough to a church
nor were we church-goers
(though we kept quiet about being communists).
The second told us
we weren't high enough earners.
The third liked us
but they had a five-year waiting list.
I spent six months trying not to look
at swings nor the front of supermarket trolleys,
not to think this kid I've wanted could be five.
The fourth agency was full up.
The fifth said yes but again no babies.
Just as we were going out the door
I said oh you know we don't mind the colour.
Just like that, the waiting was over.

This morning a slim manilla envelope arrives
postmarked Edinburgh: one piece of paper
I have now been able to look up your microfiche
(as this is all the records kept nowadays).
From your mother's letters, the following information:
Your mother was nineteen when she had you.
You weighed eight pounds four ounces.
She liked hockey. She worked in Aberdeen
as a waitress. She was five foot eight inches.

I thought I'd hid everything
that there wasnie wan
giveaway sign left

I put Marx Engels Lenin (no Trotsky)
in the airing cupboard – she'll no be
checking out the towels surely

All the copies of the *Daily Worker*
I shoved under the sofa
the dove of peace I took down from the loo

A poster of Paul Robeson
saying give him his passport
I took down from the kitchen

I left a bust of Burns
my detective stories
and the Complete Works of Shelley

She comes at 11.30 exactly.
I pour her coffee
from my new Hungarian set

And foolishly pray she willnae
ask its origins – honestly
this baby is going to my head.

She crosses her legs on the sofa
I fancy I hear the *Daily Workers*
rustle underneath her

Well she says, you have an interesting home
She sees my eyebrows rise.
It's different she qualifies.

Hell and I've spent all morning
trying to look ordinary
– a lovely home for the baby.

She buttons her coat all smiles
I'm thinking
I'm on the home run

But just as we get to the last post
her eye catches at the same times as mine
a red ribbon with twenty world peace badges

Clear as a hammer and sickle
on the wall.
Oh, she says are you against nuclear weapons?

To Hell with this. Baby or no baby.
Yes I says. Yes yes yes.
I'd like this baby to live in a nuclear free world.

Oh. Her eyes light up.
I'm all for peace myself she says,
and sits down for another cup of coffee.

In Jackie Kay's *The Adoption Papers* sequence, the voices of the three speakers
are distinguished typographically, including:

DAUGHTER: Palatino typeface
ADOPTIVE MOTHER: Gill typeface

Dance of the Cherry Blossom

Both of us are getting worse
Neither knows who had it first

He thinks I gave it to him
I think he gave it to me

83

Nights chasing clues where
One memory runs into another like dye.

Both of us are getting worse
I know I'm wasting precious time

But who did he meet between
May '87 and March '89.

I feel his breath on my back
A slow climb into himself then out.

In the morning it all seems different
Neither knows who had it first

We eat breakfast together – newspapers
And silence except for the slow slurp of tea

This companionship is better than anything
He thinks I gave it to him.

By lunchtime we're fighting over some petty thing
He tells me I've lost my sense of humour

I tell him I'm not Glaswegian
You all think death is a joke

It's not funny. I'm dying for fuck's sake
I think he gave it to me.

Just think he says it's every couple's dream
I won't have to wait for you up there

I'll have you night after night – your glorious legs
Your strong hard belly, your kissable cheeks

I cry when he says things like that
My shoulders cave in, my breathing trapped

Do you think you have a corner on dying
You self-pitying wretch, pathetic queen.

He pushes me; we roll on the floor like whirlwind;
When we are done in, our lips find each other

We touch soft as breeze, caress the small parts
Rocking back and forth, his arms become mine

There's nothing outside but the noise of the wind
The cherry blossom's dance through the night.

Pounding Rain

News of us spreads like a storm.
The top of our town to the bottom.
We stand behind curtains
parted like hoods; watch each other's eyes.

We talk of moving to the west end,
this bit has always been a shoe box
tied with string; but then again
your father still lives in that house
where we warmed up spaghetti bolognese
in lunch hours and danced to Louis Armstrong,
his gramophone loud as our two heart beats
going boom diddy boom diddy boom.

Did you know then? I started dating Davy;
when I bumped into you I'd just say Hi.
I tucked his photo booth smile into my satchel
brought him out for my pals in the intervals.

A while later I heard you married Trevor Campbell.
Each night I walked into the school dinner hall
stark naked, till I woke to Miss, Miss Miss
every minute. Then, I bumped into you at the Cross.

You haven't changed you said; that reassurance.
Nor you; your laugh still crosses the street.
I trace you back, beaming , till –
Why don't you come round, Trevor would love it.

He wasn't in. I don't know how it happened.
We didn't bother with a string of do you remembers.
I ran my fingers through the beads in your hair.
Your hair's nice I said stupidly, nice, suits you.

We sat and stared till our eyes filled
like a glass of wine. I did it, the thing
I'd dreamt a million times. I undressed you
slowly, each item of clothing fell
with a sigh. I stroked your silk skin
until we were back in the Campsies, running
down the hills in the pounding rain,
screaming and laughing; soaked right through.

The Red Graveyard

There are some stones that open in the night like flowers
Down in the red graveyard where Bessie haunts her lovers.
There are stones that shake and weep in the heart of night
Down in the red graveyard where Bessie haunts her lovers.

Why do I remember the blues?
I am five or six or seven in the back garden;
the window is wide open;
her voice is slow motion through the heavy summer air.
Jelly roll. Kitchen man. Sausage roll. Frying pan.

Inside the house where I used to be myself,
her voice claims the rooms. In the best room even,
something has changed the shape of my silence.
Why do I remember her voice and not my own mother's?
Why do I remember the blues?

My mother's voice. What was it like?
A flat stone for skitting. An old rock.
Long long grass. Asphalt. Wind. Hail.
Cotton. Linen. Salt. Treacle.
I think it was a peach.
I heard it down to the ribbed stone.

I am coming down the stairs in my father's house.
I am five or six or seven. There is fat thick wallpaper
I always caress, bumping flower into flower.
She is singing. (Did they play anyone else ever?)
My father's feet tap a shiny beat on the floor.

Christ, my father says, that's some voice she's got.
I pick up the record cover. And now. This is slow motion.
My hand swoops, glides, swoops again.
I pick up the cover and my fingers are all over her face.
Her black face. Her magnificent black face.
That's some voice. His shoes dancing on the floor.

There are some stones that open in the night like flowers
Down in the red graveyard where Bessie haunts her lovers.
There are stones that shake and weep in the heart of night
Down in the red graveyard where Bessie haunts her lovers.

Blues

Hell, I can't even take my own advice,
that's what she thought often, when her left eye
(always the left) was swollen and a blue river
ran underneath the brown; or when
whole parts of her body could not
be walked on, or swam in, or touched even.
When her body had no-go areas; something-only areas.
Danger: a fence right round her skin, wooden
as her own voice the morning after

all that violence. It was in the way they looked at her.
It was not in her mind. She did not grow such looks
in her own backyard. The hard stare; the furtive one where
the eyes were a fast car swerving as she walked near.
Nothing could persuade her not to be funny.
She could not stop being funny. Making people
laugh till they cried, hurt themselves, howl.
She was a shouter. She could barrelhouse.
But on the morning after all that violence

she could not raise the roof of her voice.
She could not embellish or endow or growl.
Laugh, yes. Grunt. Giggle. Once she caught herself
in the trembling mirror. *A minstrel.*
She tried to be completely still.

As if she were committing a murder.
A clown. An aunt jemima. She has a smile
that could cross a river. And she had a laugh
that could build a raft. And that was all she had.

Twelve Bar Bessie

See that day, Lord, did you hear what happened then.
A nine o'clock shadow always chases the sun.
And in the thick heavy air came the Ku Klux Klan
To the tent where the Queen was about to sing her song.

They were going to pull the Blues Tent down.
Going to move the Queen out of the town.
Take her twelve bar beat and squash it into the ground.
She tried to get her Prop Boys together, and they got scared.

She tried to get the Prop Boys together, and they got scared.
She said Boys, Boys, get those men out of here.
But they ran away and left the Empress on her own.
She went up to the men who had masks over their head

With her hand on her hips she cursed and she hollered,
'I'll get the whole damn lot of you out of here now
If I have to. You are as good as dead.
You just pick up the sheets and run. Go on.'

That's what she done. Her voice was cast-iron.
You should have seen them. You should have seen them.
Those masks made of sheets from somebody's bed.
Those masks flying over their heads. Flapping.

They was flapping like some strange bird migrating.
Some bird that smelt danger in the air, a blue song.
And flew. Fast. Out of the small mid western town.
To the sound of black hands clapping.

And the Empress saying, 'And as for you' to the ones who did nothing.

In my country

walking by the waters
down where an honest river
shakes hands with the sea,
a woman passed round me
in a slow watchful circle,
as if I were a superstition;

or the worst dregs of her imagination,
so when she finally spoke
her words spliced into bars
of an old wheel. A segment of air.
Where do you come from?
'Here,' I said, 'Here. These parts.'

Hottentot Venus

They made a plaster cast of my corpse
took wax moulds of my genitals and anus,
my famous anomalous buttocks
till the last sigh in me left my body.

I made a noise I never heard before
when the man with the glinting knife
whispered 'posterity' and dissected my brain.
Not so long ago people paid handsomely

to see my rump, my apron, my non-European genitals.
Two shillings. I paced my cage, backwards,
an orang outang, forwards, a beast on a chain.
Men said the size of my lips were unnatural.

You can see the moulds of my genitals
at the Musée de l'Homme – Paris;
the rest of me is here now, Natural History Museum,
my brains, my woolly hair, my skeleton.

Some things I will never forget
no matter how I am divided up:
the look on a white lady's face
when she poked her parasol into my privates.

Her gloved hands. Her small stone eyes.
Her English squeal of surprise at my size.
My sigh is black. My heart is black.
My walk is black. My hide, my flanks. My secret.

My brain is the size of a black woman's brain.
When the gentleman prodded me with his cane,
he wanted to discover black tears falling
from my dark eyes. I tell no lies.

Then he called my tears crocodile tears.
What did he call my lips? Rubber? Blubber?
My country is a dream now. Or maybe it did not exist.
When they called me in, three men in suits,

They asked me in my own bush tongue
if I wanted to be exhibited in this fashion.
I said the English words I'd heard them say often.
Money. Freedom. My Boer keeper smiled.

He could still walk me, dance me
hold his stick to me. He promised me riches.
Bring in the literati, the artists, the famous.
Let them view the buttocks of the Hottentot Venus.

My heart inside my cage pounded like a single drum.
For eleven hours a day people came to see Saartjie Baartman.
I heard their laughter like money shaking in a tin.
On the wall I was framed: ugly, deformed, a cartoon.

I was wearing a thin skin coloured dress.
Hottentot Venus. Don't miss the Hottentot.
Now, what name have I got?
Sarah Bateman. Like an English woman. A great actress.

Somebody Else

If I was not myself, I would be somebody else.
But actually I am somebody else.
I have been somebody else all my life.

It's no laughing matter going about the place
all the time being somebody else:
people mistake you; you mistake yourself.

Pride

When I looked up, the black man was there,
staring into my face,
as if he had always been there,
as if he and I went a long way back.
He looked into the dark pool of my eyes
as the train slid out of Euston.
For a long time this went on
the stranger and I looking at each other,
a look that was like something being given
from one to the other.

My whole childhood, I'm quite sure,
passed before him, the worst things
I've ever done, the biggest lies I've ever told.
And he was a little boy on a red dust road.
He stared into the dark depth of me,
and then he spoke:
'Ibo,' he said. 'Ibo, definitely.'
Our train rushed through the dark.
'You are an Ibo!' he said, thumping the table.
My coffee jumped and spilled.
Several sleeping people woke.
The night train boasted and whistled
through the English countryside,
past unwritten stops in the blackness.

'That nose is an Ibo nose.
Those teeth are Ibo teeth,' the stranger said,
his voice getting louder and louder.
I had no doubt, from the way he said it,
that Ibo noses are the best noses in the world,
that Ibo teeth are perfect pearls.
People were walking down the trembling aisle
to come and look
as the night rain babbled against the window.
There was a moment when
my whole face changed into a map,
and the stranger on the train
located even the name
of my village in Nigeria
in the lower part of my jaw.

I told him what I'd heard was my father's name.
Okafor. He told me what it meant,
something stunning,
something so apt and astonishing.
Tell me, I asked the black man on the train
who was himself transforming,
at roughly the same speed as the train,
and could have been
at any stop, my brother, my father as a young man,
or any member of my large clan,
Tell me about the Ibos.

His face had a look
I've seen on a MacLachlan, a MacDonnell, a MacLeod,
the most startling thing, pride,
a quality of being certain.
Now that I know you are an Ibo, we will eat.
He produced a spicy meat patty,
ripping it into two.
Tell me about the Ibos.
'The Ibos are small in stature
Not tall like the Yoruba or Hausa.
The Ibos are clever, reliable,
dependable, faithful, true.
The Ibos should be running Nigeria.
There would be none of this corruption.'

And what, I asked, are the Ibos faults?
I smiled my newly acquired Ibo smile,
flashed my gleaming Ibo teeth.
The train grabbed at a bend,
'Faults? No faults. Not a single one.'

'If you went back,' he said brightening,
'The whole village would come out for you.
Massive celebrations. Definitely.
Definitely,' he opened his arms wide.
'The eldest grandchild – fantastic welcome.
If the grandparents are alive.'

I saw myself arriving
the hot dust, the red road,
the trees heavy with other fruits,
the bright things, the flowers.
I saw myself watching
the old people dance towards me
dressed up for me in happy prints.
And I found my feet.
I started to dance.
I danced a dance I never knew I knew.
Words and sounds fell out of my mouth like seeds.
I astonished myself.
My grandmother was like me exactly, only darker.

When I looked up, the black man had gone.
Only my own face startled me in the dark train window.

Things Fall Apart

My birth father lifted his hands above his head
and put the white mask of God on his handsome face.

A born-again man now, gone were the old tribal ways,
the ancestral village – African chiefs' nonsense, he says.

I could see his eyes behind the hard alabaster.
A father, no more real, still less real – not Wole Soyinka.

Less flesh than dark earth; less blood than red dust.
Less bone than Kano camels; less like me than Chinua Achebe.

Christianity had scrubbed his black face with a hard brush.
'You are my past sin, let us deliberate on new birth.'

The sun slips and slides and finally drops
into the swimming pool, in Nico hotel, Abuja; lonely pinks.

I knock back my dry spritzer, take in the songs
of African birds. I think he had my hands, my father.

Late Love

How they strut about, people in love,
how tall they grow, pleased with themselves,
their hair, glossy, their skin shining.
They don't remember who they have been.

How filmic they are just for this time.
How important they've become – secret, above
the order of things, the dreary mundane.
Every church bell ringing, a fresh sign.

How dull the lot that are not in love.
Their clothes shabby, their skin lustreless;
how clueless they are, hair a mess; how they trudge
up and down streets in the rain,

remembering one kiss in a dark alley,
a touch in a changing-room, if lucky, a lovely wait
for the phone to ring, maybe, baby.
The past with its rush of velvet, its secret hush

already miles away, dimming now, in the late day.

It's You and Me Baby All the Way to the End of the Line

Yesterday you lied to me, my true love.
I knew you were, pretended you weren't –
that way maybe we could both be safer:
strolling along a disused railway line or
watching an old movie in our living-room.

Somehow yesterday it felt much better,
you lying into the home telephone;
your voice less sure now, less certain, softer.
And me here, miles away, snow on the hills,
listening to your voice down the long line

lying, love, like soft rain, lying again.
Today I can hear it still, picture, you, her
in some hotel, your voice, light in her ear.
Till I push you back further and further;
till I see nothing, just snow on the hills.

Old Tongue

When I was eight, I was forced south.
Not long after, when I opened
my mouth, a strange thing happened.
I lost my Scottish accent.
Words fell off my tongue:
eedyit, dreich, wabbit, crabbit
stummer, teuchter, heidbanger,
so you are, so am ur, see you, see ma ma,
shut yer geggie or I'll gie you the malkie!

My own vowels started to stretch like my bones
and I turned my back on Scotland.
Words disappeared in the dead of night,
new words marched in: ghastly, awful,

quite dreadful, *scones* said like *stones.*
Pokey hats into ice cream cones.
Oh where did all my words go –
my old words, my lost words?
Did you ever feel sad when you lost a word,
did you ever try and call it back
like calling in the sea?
If I could have found my words wandering,
I swear I would have taken them in,
swallowed them whole, knocked them back.

Out in the English soil, my old words
buried themselves. It made my mother's blood boil.
I cried one day with the wrong sound in my mouth.
I wanted them back; I wanted my old accent back,
my old tongue. My dour soor Scottish tongue.
Sing-songy. I wanted to *gie it laldie.*

Life Mask

When the senses come back in the morning,
the nose is a mouth full of spring;
the mouth is an earful of birdsong;
the eyes are lips on the camomile lawn;
the ear is an eye of calm blue sky.

When the broken heart begins to mend,
the heart is a bird with a tender wing,
the tears are pear blossom blossoming,
the shaken love grows green shining leaves.
the throat doesn't close, it is opening

like a long necked swan in the morning,
like the sea and the river meeting,
like the huge heron's soaring wings:
I sat up with my pale face in my hands
and all of a sudden it was spring.